AF700045

# Implicit Attitude Measures

Editors:
Melanie C. Steffens
Kai J. Jonas

Zeitschrift für Psychologie
Journal of Psychology

Vol. 218, No. 1, 2010

HOGREFE

**Library of Congress Cataloging in Publication**

is available via the Library of Congress Marc Database under the
LC Control Number 2010921354

**Library and Archives Canada Cataloguing in Publication**

Implicit attitude measures / editors, Melanie C. Steffens, Kai J. Jonas.

Published as Zeitschrift für Psychologie = Journal of psychology, vol. 218, no. 1, 2010.

Includes bibliographical references.
ISBN 978-0-88937-386-0

1. Attitude (Psychology)–Testing 2. Social psychology–Research–Methodology. I. Steffens, Melanie C., 1969- II. Jonas, Kai J.

BF327.I57 2010 152.4028'7 C2010-900701-8

© 2010 Hogrefe Publishing

PUBLISHING OFFICES
USA: Hogrefe Publishing, 875 Massachusetts Avenue, 7th Floor, Cambridge, MA 02139
Phone (866) 823-4726, Fax (617) 354-6875; E-mail customerservice@hogrefe-publishing.com
EUROPE: Hogrefe Publishing, Rohnsweg 25, 37085 Göttingen, Germany
Phone +49 551 49609-0, Fax +49 551 49609-88, E-mail publishing@hogrefe.com

SALES & DISTRIBUTION
USA: Hogrefe Publishing, Customer Services Department, 30 Amberwood Parkway, Ashland,
OH 44805, Phone (800) 228-3749, Fax (419) 281-6883, E-mail customerservice@hogrefe.com
EUROPE: Hogrefe Publishing, Rohnsweg 25, 37085 Göttingen, Germany
Phone +49 551 49609-0, Fax +49 551 49609-88, E-mail publishing@hogrefe.com

OTHER OFFICES
CANADA: Hogrefe Publishing, 660 Eglinton Ave. East, Suite 119-514, Toronto, Ontario M4G 2K2
SWITZERLAND: Hogrefe Publishing, Länggass-Strasse 76, CH-3000 Bern 9

Hogrefe Publishing
Incorporated and registered in the Commonwealth of Massachusetts, USA, and in Göttingen, Lower Saxony, Germany

No part of this publication may be reproduced, stored in a retrieval system or transmitted, in any form or by any means, electronic, mechanical, photocopying, microfilming, recording or otherwise, without written permission from the publisher.
ISBN 978-0-88937-386-0

# Contents



© 2010 Hogrefe Publishing

# Implicit Attitude Measures

Melanie C. Steffens[1] and Kai J. Jonas[2]

[1]Friedrich Schiller University, Jena, Germany
[2]University of Amsterdam, The Netherlands

Arguably, one of the most thriving research areas in current psychology is assessing attitudes and related constructs with implicit measures, which we define as those indirect measures that rely on response latencies or other indices of spontaneous trait association, the activation of action semantics, or even real behavior. This research area is united by a shared excitement about the discoveries enabled by these measures, be they related to social attitudes and behavior, clinical disorders, consumer decisions, or self-representations, among others. As this enumeration suggests, in spite of the common excitement about the new research questions implicit measures allow us to investigate, there is much diversity in this research. First of all, these approaches bridge subdisciplines of psychology traditionally characterized by little cross-talk. Furthermore, the variety of implicit measures used is already broad and still growing, given variants and implementations of these implicit measures in different samples and research approaches. Given this diversity, we deemed it appropriate to summarize research that focuses either on the comparison of different implicit measures or on the mechanisms underlying one of the measures. Such knowledge is necessary and helpful to determine which measure to employ in a given research context and also to be aware of limitations of certain measures and advantages of others. Thus, the articles collected in this special issue compare two or more different implicit measures, or they focus on the measurement properties of one.

One of the mostly used implicit measures, the Implicit Association Test (IAT; Greenwald, McGhee, & Schwartz, 1998), was introduced in a way that would have allowed researchers to implement it as if it was a standardized test. In spite of this, researchers not only used stimuli, numbers of trials, evaluation procedures, and other specifics different from those suggested; but in the end, they even suggested their own variants of IATs or implicit measures that keep certain aspects of IATs while eliminating or adding others (e.g., De Houwer, 2003; Nosek & Banaji, 2001; Olson & Fazio, 2004; Sriram & Greenwald, 2009; Steffens, Kirschbaum, & Glados, 2008). As a first consequence, the answer to the question how a "good" IAT should be constructed is not as clean and tidy anymore as it appeared in 1998. As a second consequence of these methodological debates IAT research now comprises a diversity at the expense of addressing comparisons with other implicit measures (the implicit-explicit relation on the contrary has been attended to, e.g., Hofmann, Gawronski, Gschwendner, Le, & Schmitt, 2005).

Matters get much more complicated if we add other implicit measures to this cocktail, the most prominent ones among them being based on priming effects (Fazio, Sanbonmatsu, Powell, & Kardes, 1986; Payne, Cheng, Govorun, & Stewart, 2005), but many recent ones based on approach-avoidance reactions (see Reinecke, Becker, & Rinck, 2010). Whereas some research has systematically compared different implicit measures and found disturbing discrepancies among them (e.g., Bosson, Swann, & Pennebaker, 2000) and among the mechanisms underlying them (e.g., Gawronski & Bodenhausen, 2005; Wittenbrink, Judd, & Park, 2001), such research is the exception rather than the rule, compared to the enormous number of studies applying implicit measures. On top of that, some types of implicit measures have not yet reached a consolidation level that would allow these comparisons, but are still dealing with the analysis of the robustness and determinants of the respective effects. For instance, this is the case for automatic behavior activation following categorical primes where it still needs to be figured out what kind of behavior is being activated and when (Jonas & Sassenberg, 2006). Consequently, we believe that few informed decisions can be made which implicit measure is most appropriate for a given research question. Of course, this is not to say that we know nothing. For instance, we know that a measure such as subliminal priming is preferable if we want to assess social cognition in the absence of conscious perception of stimuli, and such measures may yield reliable interindividual differences (e.g., Bianchi, Mummendey, Steffens, & Yzerbyt, in press). On the contrary, we know that even if participants do not control their responses during an IAT, they will afterwards have a pretty clear idea which constructs were assessed (e.g., Steffens, 2004), thus, the latter measures are certainly less implicit than the former (cf. Dasgupta, 2010). Whereas we know that subliminal measures may yield replicable effects (Draine & Greenwald, 1998), it is possible that they yield less reliable findings than other measures. So what we do not know is under what conditions and for which research questions an IAT outperforms a priming paradigm or an approach-avoidance dependent measure, and vice versa. For example, when there was no consensus on the

© 2010 Hogrefe Publishing
*Zeitschrift für Psychologie / Journal of Psychology* 2010; Vol. 218(1):1–3
DOI: 10.1027/0044-3409/a000001

best implicit measure to use, a group from our laboratory decided on a pretest. Much to our surprise, a subliminal affective priming measure showed the best validity, so it was used in the main experiment, and with success (Heigener, Martiny, Steffens, & Kessler, 2009).

Similarly, we need to know to which research questions a given measure can be applied in principle, and which are precluded due to features of the measure. Which findings can be interpreted with regard to implicitly assessed cognition, and which reflect features of the measure instead? Thus, experiments are badly needed in the field that focus on the features of the measures themselves, and those directly comparing the strengths and weaknesses of different implicit measures against each other.

Ironically, it appears that there is some publication bias against these studies that we consider vital. Whereas in cognitive psychology, there is consensus that it is theoretical progress to understand how response-compatibility effects or negative priming effects come about, in social psychology reviewers and editors often seem to detect "no contribution to theory" if a mechanism underlying an implicit measure is investigated (cf. also Degner, Wentura, & Rothermund, 2006). At the same time, cognitive journals often regard research on implicit attitude measures as appropriate for the journals of the outgroup (i.e., social psychologists). These are the main reasons why we were happy to edit a special issue on implicit attitude measures. The number of abstracts and submissions we received corroborates the timeliness of the idea.

Reflecting the diversity in the field, the articles in the present issue target attitudes toward social groups (Blair, Judd, Havranek, & Steiner, 2010; Popa-Roch & Delmas, 2010; von Stülpnagel & Steffens, 2010), self-attitudes (Popa-Roch & Delmas, 2010; Rudolph, Schröder-Abè, Riketta, & Schütz, 2010), consumer attitudes (Summerville, Hsieh, & Harrington, 2010), attitudes toward spiders (Reinecke et al., 2010), and those toward risk taking (Dislich, Zinkernagel, Ortner, & Schmitt, 2010). The hope underlying these investigations is that general conclusions about the respective measures can be drawn from their specific instantiations.

So what can we learn from the research collected in this issue? Reinecke and colleagues demonstrated encouraging reliabilities and validities for three very different implicit tasks. Particularly impressive were the obtained correlations with a behavioral measure (approaching a spider), all the more so as the sample consisted of university students with no clinical comparison groups that would increase variance. Implicit measures thus provide valuable additions to clinicians' toolboxes. Similarly, using a double-dissociation approach, Rudolph et al. showed that implicit measures of self-esteem predict spontaneous behavior. This was true both for an IAT and a new measure capitalizing on self-judgments under cognitive load. Using a similar approach, the findings reported by Dislich et al. are compatible with the view that implicit (here: an IAT) and explicit measures predict different aspects of risk taking behavior.

These studies converge on finding indicators of the quality of different implicit measures, instead of demonstrating the superiority of one measure over another. It thus appears that for many research questions, it does not play a major role which implicit measure one chooses. Going beyond this, Summerville and colleagues showed that two different implicit measures, evaluative movement assessment and evaluative priming, were related to each other, but not to purchase intentions, which were however predicted by a lexical decision task. In other words, these findings point at the differential validity of different implicit measures, a fruitful avenue for future research.

As is quite common, the current studies focusing on only a single implicit measure investigated IATs. The findings mirror both sides of the debate on IATs' validity. Blair et al. add considerable weight to the evidence that IAT effects reflect what they are supposed to, demonstrating their discriminant validity. It is subject to debate whether the main finding of Popa-Roch and Dumas speaks against the validity of IATs or not, namely that apparent negative attitudes toward an outgroup can be based on positive attitudes toward the self (i.e., an ingroup member; cf. Dasgupta, 2010). In contrast, a short report by von Stülpnagel and Steffens points at a potential threat to IATs' validity by showing that IAT effects are sometimes correlated with intelligence measures in the direction opposite to that suggested by explicit prejudice measures. Taken together, these findings are compatible with the view that IATs contain a large portion of variance related to the purpose of measurement (e.g., attitudes), but that some of their variance is related to other constructs. We want to hasten to add that the same may be true for other implicit measures, and this will go undiscovered until they are investigated with the same scrutiny as IATs are. Similarly, the present and other findings show that there is no reason to automatically prefer IATs to other implicit measures independent of the research question. The current issue closes with a commentary by Dasgupta who, among other things, elaborates on "The next generation of unresolved questions." In a nutshell, we hope to fuel both the diversity in our research field with the current issue and at the same time highlight existing knowledge on the interrelations of implicit measures.

### Acknowledgments

The writing of this article and the compiling of the special issue were supported by a grant from the German Research Foundation DFG (Ste 938/9-1) to both authors.

## References

Bianchi, M., Mummendey, A., Steffens, M. C., & Yzerbyt, V. (in press). What do you mean by European? Evidence of spontaneous ingroup projection. *Personality and Social Psychology Bulletin*.

Blair, I. V., Judd, C. M., Havranek, E. P., & Steiner, J. F. (2010). Using community data to test the discriminate validity of ethnic/racial group IATs. *Zeitschrift für Psychologie / Journal of Psychology, 218*, 36–43.

Bosson, J. K., Swann, W. B. Jr., & Pennebaker, J. W. (2000). Stalking the perfect measure of implicit self-esteem: The blind men and the elephant revisited? *Journal of Personality and Social Psychology, 79*, 631–643.

 © 2010 Hogrefe Publishing

Dasgupta, N. (2010). Implicit measures of social cognition: Common themes and unresolved questions. *Zeitschrift für Psychologie / Journal of Psychology, 218*, 54–57.

Degner, J., Wentura, D., & Rothermund, K. (2006). Indirect assessment of attitudes with response-time-based measures. *Zeitschrift für Sozialpsychologie, 37*, 131–139.

De Houwer, J. (2003). The extrinsic affective Simon task. *Experimental Psychology, 50*, 77–85.

Dislich, F. X. R., Zinkernagel, A., Ortner, T. M., & Schmitt, M. (2010). Convergence of direct, indirect, and objective risk taking measures in the domain of gambling: The moderating role of impulsiveness and self-control. *Zeitschrift für Psychologie / Journal of Psychology, 218*, 20–27.

Draine, S. C., & Greenwald, A. G. (1998). Replicable unconscious semantic priming. *Journal of Experimental Psychology: General, 127*, 286–303.

Fazio, R. H., Sanbonmatsu, D. M., Powell, M. C., & Kardes, F. R. (1986). On the automatic activation of attitudes. *Journal of Personality and Social Psychology, 50*, 229–238.

Gawronski, B., & Bodenhausen, G. V. (2005). Accessibility effects on implicit social cognition: The role of knowledge activation and retrieval experiences. *Journal of Personality and Social Psychology, 89*, 672.

Greenwald, A. G., McGhee, D. E., & Schwartz, J. L. K. (1998). Measuring individual differences in implicit cognition: The Implicit Association Test. *Journal of Personality and Social Psychology, 74*, 1464–1480.

Heigener, M., Martiny, S., Steffens, M. C., & Kessler, T. (2009). Implicit and explicit group-based self-esteem – Dynamics in the prediction of in-group bias and identity management strategies. *Poster presented at the 51. Tagung experimentell arbeitender Psycholog|innen, Jena,* March 29–April 1, 2009.

Hofmann, W., Gawronski, B., Gschwendner, T., Le, H., & Schmitt, M. (2005). A meta-analysis on the correlation between the Implicit Association Test and explicit self-report measures. *Personality and Social Psychology Bulletin, 31*, 1369–1385.

Jonas, K. J., & Sassenberg, K. (2006). Knowing how to react: Automatic response priming from social categories. *Journal of Personality and Social Psychology, 90*, 709–721.

Nosek, B. A., & Banaji, M. R. (2001). The Go/No-go Association Task. *Social Cognition, 19*, 625–666.

Olson, M. A., & Fazio, R. H. (2004). Reducing the influence of extrapersonal associations on the Implicit Association Test: Personalizing the IAT. *Journal of Personality and Social Psychology, 86*, 653–667.

Payne, B. K., Cheng, C. M., Govorun, O., & Stewart, B. D. (2005). An inkblot for attitudes: Affect misattribution as implicit measurement. *Journal of Personality and Social Psychology, 89*, 277–293.

Popa-Roch, M., & Delmas, F. (2010). Prejudice IAT effects: The role of self-related heuristics. *Zeitschrift für Psychologie / Journal of Psychology, 218*, 44–50.

Reinecke, A., Becker, E. S., & Rinck, M. (2010). Test-retest reliability and validity of three indirect tasks assessing implicit threat associations and behavioral response tendencies. *Zeitschrift für Psychologie / Journal of Psychology, 218*, 4–11.

Rudolph, A., Schröder-Abè, M., Riketta, M., & Schütz, A. (2010). Easier when done than said! Implicit self-esteem predicts observed or spontaneous behavior, but not self-reported or controlled behavior. *Zeitschrift für Psychologie / Journal of Psychology, 218*, 12–19.

Sriram, N., & Greenwald, A. G. (2009). The brief Implicit Association Test. *Experimental Psychology, 56*, 283–294.

Steffens, M. C. (2004). Is the Implicit Association Test immune to faking? *Experimental Psychology, 51*, 165–179.

Steffens, M. C., Kirschbaum, M., & Glados, P. (2008). Avoiding stimulus confounds in Implicit Association Tests by using the concepts as stimuli. *British Journal of Social Psychology, 47*, 217–243.

Summerville, A., Hsieh, B., & Harrington, N. (2010). A multi-measure investigation of the divergence of implicit and explicit consumer evaluations. *Zeitschrift für Psychologie / Journal of Psychology, 218*, 28–35.

von Stülpnagel, R., & Steffens, M. C. (2010). Prejudiced or just smart? Intelligence as a confounding factor in the IAT effect. *Zeitschrift für Psychologie / Journal of Psychology, 218*, 51–53.

Wittenbrink, B., Judd, C. M., & Park, B. (2001). Evaluative versus conceptual judgments in automatic stereotyping and prejudice. *Journal of Experimental Social Psychology, 37*, 244–252.

Melanie C. Steffens

Institut für Psychologie
Friedrich-Schiller-Universität Jena
Am Steiger 3
Haus 1
D-07743 Jena
Germany
Tel. +49 3641 945111
Fax +49 3641 945112
E-mail melanie.steffens@uni-jena.de

© 2010 Hogrefe Publishing

Original Article

# Three Indirect Tasks Assessing Implicit Threat Associations and Behavioral Response Tendencies

## Test-Retest Reliability and Validity

Andrea Reinecke,[1] Eni S. Becker,[2] and Mike Rinck[2]

[1]Dresden University of Technology, Germany
[2]Behavioral Science Institute, Radboud University Nijmegen, The Netherlands

**Abstract.** Anxiety disorders are characterized by biased implicit threat associations, which can be measured by indirect reaction time tasks. These tasks might provide a useful tool in the assessment of individual diagnoses and therapeutic changes. However, sufficient psychometric properties of the applied tasks are a prerequisite for these applications. Therefore, we comparatively investigated the reliability and validity of an Extrinsic Affective Simon Task (EAST), an Approach-Avoidance Task (AAT), and an Affective Priming Task (APT) by presenting the same tasks twice within 1 week. Data show retest reliabilities of around $r = .42$ for the EAST, $r = .35$ for the AAT, and $r = .63$ for the APT. Internal consistencies varied between .44 and .49 for the EAST, .66 and .70 for the AAT, and .53 and .76 for the APT. Validity correlations with self-report questionnaires ranged between $r = .43$ and $r = .59$, being lowest for the EAST and highest for the AAT. We argue that while these instruments might not be applicable to individual diagnostics yet, they are sufficiently reliable and valid to be used in the assessment of group differences.

**Keywords:** implicit associations, indirect tasks, reliability, validity, threat

Fear-relevant stimuli are processed preferably and very quickly (e.g., LeDoux, 1996; Öhman, 1993). Following network theories, this phenomenon is based on particularly strong memory associations of these stimuli with the concepts of *danger*, *fear*, and related *behavioral avoidance* responses in an internal fear network (Beck, Emery, & Greenberg, 1985). Therefore, anxiety and avoidance tendencies can be activated particularly easily in anxiety patients – even by the mere thought or a picture of the threatening stimulus.

Clinical research has revealed disorder-related biases of attention (Mathews & MacLeod, 2005), working memory (Reinecke, Rinck, & Becker, 2006, 2008), and long-term memory (Coles & Heimberg, 2002) in many anxiety disorders. However, it is not clear which role biased implicit fear associations play in the etiology of anxiety disorders. During the last decade, indirect association tasks measuring these automatic, implicit evaluation processes received growing attention (De Houwer & de Bruycker, 2007), and they have recently been used to assess fear associations in clinical disorders (Ellwart, Rinck, & Becker, 2006; De Jong, Pasman, Kindt, & van den Hout, 2001; Teachman & Woody, 2003), based on the hope that these tasks are able to assess implicit evaluations difficult to measure using standard tools. Moreover, indirect tasks should be more difficult to fake than direct ones (Langner et al., in press), and they should provide additional value in predicting behavior, which is interesting in a clinical context, for instance, when trying to predict treatment success. Nevertheless, only little is known about the psychometric quality of these tasks, even though sufficient reliability and validity are necessary for any successful application of the tasks. In particular, good retest reliability is indispensable for clinical treatment studies which aim to measure changes in implicit associations or behavioral response tendencies.

For several *Priming Tasks* assessing racial stereotyping and self-esteem, the psychometric properties have been assessed. For subliminal prime presentation, 1-week retest reliability scores of .06 (Banse, 1999), .28 (Banse, 1999; Bosson, Swann, & Pennerbaker, 2000), and .50 (Kawakami & Dovidio, 2001) are reported. Supraliminal presentation was related to scores of .08 (Bosson et al., 2000), .13 (Cunningham, Preacher, & Banaji, 2001), and .60 (Kawakami & Dovidio, 2001). Studies of the psychometric properties of the *Extrinsic Affective Simon Task* (*EAST*) (De Houwer, 2003) also mainly addressed attitudes or self-concept (De Houwer, 2003; De Houwer & de Bruycker, 2007; Teige, Schnabel, Banse, & Asendorpf, 2004). They often report low internal consistency, calculated as the correlation of the first and second half of the test, with Cronbach's $\alpha$ ranging between .02 and .43. One study using an EAST to assess


© 2010 Hogrefe Publishing
DOI: 10.1027/0044-3409/a000002

general anxiety-specific self-concept (Schmuckle & Egloff, 2006) found an internal consistency between .12 and .68. The internal consistency scores for a spider anxiety EAST (Huijding & de Jong, 2005) ranged between −.57 and .56, and convergent validity scores between −.34 and .38 (Huijding & de Jong, 2009). EAST studies assessing attitudes toward alcohol report internal consistency scores between .48 and .69 (Birch et al., 2008; De Jong, Wiers, van de Braak, & Huijding, 2007) and convergent validity parameters between .37 and .38 (De Jong et al., 2007).

In sum, results concerning the psychometric properties of indirect tasks assessing trait measures lack coherence. This suggests that there is not *a single* psychometric pattern for *the* EAST or *the* Priming Task. Instead, each individual task requires its own evaluation, and we can hardly generalize from the properties of one task to those of an altered version. Also, only a few studies were designed to directly compare psychometric parameters of several different implicit measures. In addition, no study addressed the psychometric properties of an *Affective Priming Task* (APT) using threat-related materials or the psychometric parameters of an *Approach-Avoidance Task* (AAT) addressing behavioral tendencies.

The present paper aims at filling these gaps. We determined the psychometric properties of three indirect tasks, all measuring implicit associations and behavioral tendencies with phobic pictorial material. In Study 1, we assessed retest reliability and validity of a spider-related EAST (De Houwer, 2003) and an AAT (Rinck & Becker, 2007). In the *EAST*, participants first learned a positive versus a negative association with either one of two response keys. In the main experiment, they were asked to classify pictures of spiders and butterflies with respect to the animal's gaze direction as either to the right or to the left with the same two response keys. Thus, there are compatible trials in which spiders have to be classified with the "negative" key and butterflies with the "positive" key, and incompatible trials in which participants need to choose the "positive" key for spiders and the "negative" key for butterflies. Previous research with the EAST paradigm found prolonged reaction times (RTs; Ellwart, Becker, & Rinck, 2005) or increased error rates (Huijding & de Jong, 2005) in incompatible trials. In the *AAT*, behavior tendencies are tested. Participants are instructed to classify pictures of spiders and butterflies with respect to their format as either portrait or landscape by pushing the picture away or pulling it closer, by means of a joystick. Spider fearfuls find it more difficult to pull a spider picture toward themselves, leading to response delays (Rinck & Becker, 2007). In Study 2, reliability and validity of an APT (De Houwer, Hermans, Rothermund, & Wentura, 2002; Fazio, Sanbonmatsu, Powell, & Kardes, 1986) were assessed. In this *APT*, participants classified words as related either to anxiety or to pleasure. The supraliminal, incompatible presentation of a spider picture before a positive word is expected to cause slower reactions by spider fearfuls.

In order to increase the comparability of the three indirect tasks, we used the same pictorial and verbal materials in all of them. Moreover, all tasks were indirect, in that the dimension of interest (contents of the pictures: spiders vs. butterflies) was task irrelevant: Participants reacted to the gaze direction of all animals (EAST), to the format of all pictures (AAT), or they did not react to the pictures at all (APT).

## Study 1

In Study 1, we determined the psychometric properties of a spider EAST (De Houwer, 2003) and a spider AAT (Rinck & Becker, 2007) in an unselected group of participants who varied naturally in the degree of their spider anxiety. While the EAST was designed to assess threat associations, the AAT was used to measure the behavioral response tendencies of approach and avoidance.

### Methods

#### General Aspects

##### Participants

Seventy-five university students (55 women/20 men; age: $M = 22.1$, $SD = 2.6$) participated. All were without history of psychiatric disorders and had normal or corrected-to-normal vision. In return for participation, they received course credit or a payment of €10.

##### Procedure

Each participant was tested twice, with the same procedure in both sessions (interval 3–21 days and Ø 9 days). Only at the first session, students completed the trait form of the *State-Trait Anxiety Inventory* (STAI-T; Laux, Glanzmann, Schaffner, & Spielberger, 1981). In both sessions, the *Spider Anxiety Screening* (SAS; Rinck, Bundschuh, Engler, Müller, Wissmann, Ellwart, & Becker, 2002) and the *Fear of Spiders Questionnaire* (FSQ; Szymanski & O'Donohue, 1995; see Rinck et al., 2002) were then given, before completing the AAT and the EAST. Afterwards, participants completed the *Questionnaire for Depression Diagnosis* (FDD-DSM-IV: Zimmermann, Coryell, Wilson, & Corenthal, 1986; German version: Kuehner, 1997). They then filled out the *Body Sensations Questionnaire* (BSQ; Chambless, Caputo, Bright, & Gallagher, 1984; German version: Ehlers, Margraf, & Chambless, 1993) to report their physical sensations during the prior confrontation with a tarantula carapace.[1] In the subsequent *BAT*, participants'

[1] A carapace is the outer, protective covering of a tarantula which is regularly shed during maturing and looks very much like a tarantula itself.

© 2010 Hogrefe Publishing

speed in approaching a cage with a living tarantula was measured. Each session took about 60 min.

### EAST

#### Materials and Apparatus

Stimuli were 10 pleasant (e.g., happiness and pleasure) and 10 unpleasant words (e.g., fear and dangerous) in font size 24, as well as 5 photographs of spiders and 5 photographs of butterflies (300 × 400 pixels). Each picture existed in its original form and as a mirror image, such that the animal's head once tended to the right side and once to the left side.

#### Procedure

First, participants performed two practice blocks. In a *valence practice block* (80 trials), single words were categorized as either pleasant or unpleasant by pressing a left or a right key. Thereby, the two response keys were associated with an extrinsic meaning as a pleasant versus an unpleasant key. This assignment persisted during the whole experiment. Key assignment was counterbalanced across participants. In the 20 trials of the following *direction practice block*, 5 photographs of dragonflies were presented repeatedly, and participants classified the animals' gaze direction as either left (left response key) or right.

The subsequent *experimental block* consisted of 400 trials in random order. Half of the trials consisted of valence words (valence trials), the other half of animal pictures (target trials). Half of the words were pleasant and the other half unpleasant, while half of the pictures showed a spider versus a butterfly. For both animals, half of them looked to the left and the other half to the right. The 200 picture trials were of main interest: Half of them were compatible (butterflies: pleasant key and spiders: unpleasant key), the other half incompatible.

### AAT

#### Materials and Apparatus

Eight pictures of spiders, 8 pictures of butterflies, and empty frames of the size of the pictures were used. Each of the photographs existed twice, once in portrait format (400 × 300 pixels) and once in landscape format (300 × 400 pixels), yielding a total of 16 spider and 16 butterfly stimuli.

#### Procedure

Half of the participants received instructions to quickly pull the joystick when a picture in landscape format was presented and to push in view of a picture in portrait format. The other half of participants was reversely instructed. The manual joystick movement was visually supported: pictures gradually shrank when the joystick was pushed and gradually grew in size when the joystick was pulled. Participants performed 18 practice trials with landscape versus portrait empty frames to familiarize themselves with the response procedure. Afterwards, they performed two experimental blocks, separated by a break. Each of the two blocks started and ended with the presentation of 32 empty frame trials for individual calibration of joystick reactions. In between, 160 mixed trials were presented per block, each including 64 spiders, 64 butterflies, and 32 empty frames in random order with the restriction that no picture would be repeated on consecutive trials. Each picture type was presented in landscape format in half of the trials and in portrait format in the other half of trials. Thus, a pull versus push response was required in one half of the trials each. This resulted in 128 compatible trials (64 × pulling a butterfly and 64 × pushing a spider) and 128 incompatible trials (64 × pushing a butterfly and 64 × pulling a spider). Each trial was started by pressing a button on the joystick.

## Results

*EAST effects* were calculated for the spider pictures separately for each participant and test time by subtracting the median RT to spiders with the "pleasant key" from the median RT to these pictures with the "unpleasant key." A negative score indicates a negative association, a positive score a positive one. *AAT effects* were calculated by first subtracting the median RT for pulling the spider pictures from the median RT for pushing them. Afterwards, AAT effects for empty frames were individually subtracted from these values to correct for general individual joystick response tendencies. A negative AAT score indicates a relative avoidance reaction to spiders, while a positive score indicates a relative approach reaction. The *BAT speed* was calculated in meters per second. Internal consistencies were computed as Cronbach's $\alpha$ using the different pictures as items. Test-retest reliabilities were calculated as the Pearson correlation between the two repetitions of each task. Convergent validity was determined by correlating experimental scores with direct measures (spider anxiety questionnaires) as well as with a measure of behavior (speed in approaching a living spider).

### Means, Test-Retest Reliability, and Internal Consistency

#### Questionnaires and BAT

For the sample, a mean STAI-T score of 40.6 (*SD* = 4.3) and an FDD score of 6.4 (*SD* = 5.2) were calculated. Both fell within the normal range and did not compromise interpretation of the results reported below. The scores of the questionnaires SAS, FSQ, and BSQ, see Table 1, show that participants were, on average, only slightly fearful of spiders, and that there was considerable variation in level of fear. In line with previous research (e.g., Rinck et al.,

 © 2010 Hogrefe Publishing

*Table 1.* Mean values and standard deviations at the first (*T1*) and second (*T2*) test session and test-retest reliabilities in Study 1, separately for the questionnaires, BAT scores, EAST scores, and AAT scores

| Instrument | *T1* | *T2* | Retest reliability |
|---|---|---|---|
| *Questionnaires* | | | |
| SAS | 9.6 (7.1) | 6.9 (7.3) | .89*** |
| FSQ | 22.0 (25.5) | 18.9 (25.9) | .95*** |
| BSQ | 24.0 (9.8) | 20.8 (6.4) | .88*** |
| *Behavioral approach test* | | | |
| BAT Speed | 0.7 (0.4) | 1.0 (0.5) | .84*** |
| *Experimental tasks* | | | |
| EAST effect spiders | −1 (46) | −3 (35) | .42*** |
| AAT effect spiders | −27 (104) | −1 (73) | .35** |

*Note.* $^{**}p < 0.01$, $^{***}p < 0.001$.

2002), very good to excellent retest reliabilities were determined for all questionnaires, SAS: $r = .89$, FSQ: $r = .95$, BSQ: $r = .88$; all $p < .001$, and for the speed in approaching a living tarantula, $r = .84$, $p < .001$.

### Experimental Tasks

Regarding *EAST effects* at the first test (see Table 1), we observed a positive association with butterflies, $t(74) = 2.06$, $p < .05$, $d = 0.34$, and a neutral association with spiders, $t(74) < 1$, leading to a marginally significant difference between the two associations, $t(74) = 1.78$, $p = .08$, $d = 0.48$. At the second test, associations with both picture types were neutral, butterflies: $t(74) = 1.51$, $p = .14$, spiders: $t(74) < 1$, but still marginally different from each other, $t(74) = 1.83$, $p = .07$, $d = 0.12$. For the spider EAST effect, retest reliability was low, but still highly significant, $r = .42$, $p < .001$. Internal consistency was $\alpha = .44$ at the first test and .49 at the second test.

Regarding *AAT effects* at the first test, response tendencies toward butterflies were significantly more positive than for spiders, $t(74) = 2.40$, $p < .05$, $d = 0.29$. We observed a neutral response tendency for butterfly pictures, $t(74) = 0.21$, $p = .84$, and an avoidance tendency for spiders, $t(74) = 2.29$, $p < .05$, $d = 0.37$. While the response tendency toward butterflies remained stable from the first to the second test, $t(74) = 0.69$, $p = .50$, the avoidance response for spiders was significantly weaker at the second test, $t(74) = 2.20$, $p < .05$, $d = 0.29$. For the spider AAT effect, retest reliability was $r = .35$, $p < .01$. Cronbach's $\alpha$ varied between .66 (first test) and .70 (second test).

## Validity

### Effect Scores and Questionnaires

The *spider EAST effect* and the *spider AAT effect* significantly correlated with the FSQ, the SAS, and the BSQ at both test sessions, see the left part of Table 2. The EAST effect correlations with self-reported spider anxiety lay approximately between −.20 and −.30 (all $p < .05$), that is, higher questionnaire scores predicted more negative associations. The AAT effect correlations with spider anxiety ranged from −.45 to −.59 (all $p < .001$), that is, higher questionnaire scores predicted more avoidance. AAT effect correlations at the second test were slightly lower than at the first test. For both EAST effects and AAT effects, correlations with the BSQ were at about −.30 (all $p < .05$).

### Effect Scores and BAT Scores

Negative associations with spiders (EAST) and spider avoidance tendencies (AAT) were related to lower speed in the BAT, yielding correlations between $r = .27$ and $r = .43$ (all $p < .05$). At the first test, the correlation was slightly higher for the AAT effect than for the EAST effect. However, the correlation with the AAT effect was reduced at the second test. Interestingly, the two indirect tasks predicted approach speed almost independently of each other, as evidenced by partial correlations. Controlling for the EAST, the AAT-Speed correlations were hardly reduced ($r = .40$

*Table 2.* Correlations of questionnaires and BAT scores with EAST and AAT effect scores in Study 1 (left), and with the priming effect in Study 2 (right)

| | Study 1 | | | | Study 2 | |
|---|---|---|---|---|---|---|
| | *T1* | | *T2* | | *T1* | *T2* |
| Tests | EAST spider | AAT spider | EAST spider | AAT spider | Priming effect | Priming effect |
| *T1* AAT | .15 | – | – | – | | |
| *T2* AAT | – | – | .30** | – | | |
| SAS | −.23* | −.54*** | −.31** | −.45*** | .31** | .26* |
| FSQ | −.32** | −.59*** | −.33** | −.49*** | .42*** | .41*** |
| BSQ | −.30** | −.37*** | −.31** | −.29* | .30* | .39*** |
| BAT speed | .28* | .43*** | .27* | .30** | −.39*** | −.24* |

*Note.* $^{*}p < 0.05$, $^{**}p < 0.01$, $^{***}p < 0.001$.

© 2010 Hogrefe Publishing

and .24, both $p < .05$). Similarly, the EAST-Speed correlations remained similar, even after controlling for the AAT ($r = .24$ and .19).

## Discussion

For the *EAST*, we determined an acceptable[2] retest reliability of $r = .42$. Previous studies only reported internal consistency scores (De Houwer, 2003; Huijding & de Jong, 2005), fairly similar to our own findings of $\alpha = .44$ and .49. The validity scores of the EAST, although statistically significant, were rather low. Nevertheless, the EAST effect was significantly related to self-reported spider fear, physiological strain during confrontation, and slower approach to a living spider in the BAT at both test sessions. Although comparable to an earlier spider EAST study (Huijding & de Jong, 2009), the low scores seem surprising at first, given that the reliability of the EAST was acceptable. It may be that the EAST is more sensitive to negative spider associations which are widespread in the population (hardly anybody associates spiders with positive attributes; see Ellwart et al., 2006), rather than to subtle differences in the strength of these negative associations. For the *AAT*, retest reliability was slightly lower than that for the EAST, while internal consistency was higher. Validity scores were also slightly higher for the AAT than for the EAST, but still far from what is conventionally considered satisfying. Moreover, the two tasks barely shared any variance. The partial correlations reported above suggest that, as expected, they assess different aspects of the fear schema, namely threat associations in the EAST versus behavioral response tendencies in the AAT.

# Study 2

In Study 2, reliability and validity were assessed for an APT (De Houwer et al., 2002; Fazio et al., 1986) involving the same materials as in Study 1.

## Methods

Methods were identical to Study 1 with the following exceptions.

### General Aspects

#### Participants, Materials, and Apparatus

Sixty-nine students (58 women and 11 men; age: $M = 20.8$ and $SD = 2.3$) participated in the study. The stimuli were 8 pleasant and 8 unpleasant words. Four photographs of butterflies and four images of spiders were used as originals and mirror images.

#### Procedure

An *APT* was applied instead of an EAST or an AAT. Due to time restrictions, only the prescreening and the priming task were presented during the second test session, yielding a 40-min and a 25-min test session. In each experimental trial, a fixation cross was directly followed by either a spider or a butterfly prime, presented for 200 ms. Afterwards, a target word was presented for at most 5000 ms. Participants classified it as either pleasant or unpleasant as quickly and accurately as possible (with key assignment counterbalanced across participants), and were instructed to merely watch the pictures for a later test. After four practice trials with stimuli different from those used in the later test, participants performed 256 trials divided into 10 blocks. In half of the trials, the target word required a positive response, in the other half a negative response. Both pleasant and unpleasant words were preceded by a spider picture or a butterfly picture on half of the trials. Thus, there were 128 compatible trials (64 × butterfly and pleasant word and 64 × spider and unpleasant word) and 128 incompatible trials.

## Results

### Means, Retest Reliability, and Internal Consistencies

#### Questionnaires and BAT Scores

STAI-T ($M = 45.1$ and $SD = 26.0$) and FDD score ($M = 8.5$ and $SD = 6.6$) fell within normal range. Mean self-reported spider anxiety was 11.8 ($SD = 5.9$) on the SAS, and 26.1 ($SD = 24.6$) on the FSQ. The mean BSQ score was 25.7 ($SD = 9.2$). On average, participants approached the tarantula at 0.51 ($SD = 0.26$) meters per second during the BAT.

#### Experimental Task

The three-way ANOVA with the factors target, prime, and test time revealed a large priming effect, indicated by a significant Prime × Target interaction $F(1, 68) = 40.2$, $p < .001$, $d = 1.53$: On average, the two incompatible combinations yielded longer RTs than the two compatible ones. This priming effect was significant at both the first test, $F(1, 68) = 34.6$, $p < .001$, $d = 1.44$; and the second test, $F(1, 68) = 30.5$, $p < .001$, $d = 1.34$. It was slightly stronger during the first test than during the second one, as evidenced by a significant three-way interaction, $F(1, 68) = 7.72$, $p < .01$, $d = 0.67$. For the correlational analyses, priming effects were calculated according to the standard procedure:

[2] Note that this evaluation is based on a comparison with other RT measures, not with self-report measures. This issue is discussed in the General Discussion section.

 © 2010 Hogrefe Publishing

For each participant, the average RT for the two compatible conditions (negative target word after spider prime and positive target word after butterfly prime) was subtracted from the average RT for the two incompatible conditions (negative target after butterfly prime and positive target after spider prime). The larger this priming effect is, the more negative are the measured associations. Therefore, we expect positive correlations of this priming effect with other measures of spider anxiety. The mean priming effect was 86 ms ($SD$ = 122) for the first test and 54 ms ($SD$ = 82) for the second test. Retest reliability for the priming effect was good, $r = .63$, $p < .001$. Cronbach's $\alpha$ was .75 at the first test and .53 at the second test.

### Validity

As shown in the right part of Table 2, large priming effects at the first and second test were positively related to high self-reported fear of spiders (SAS and FSQ) at the first test, to self-reported physiological strain in view of a spider carapace, and to slower approach of a living spider (all $r > .24$, all $p < .05$).

## Discussion

The APT showed good[2] retest reliability, internal consistency, and validity. Compared to the EAST and AAT, the *APT* revealed the highest retest reliability of all three tasks, yielding $r = .63$. This is in line with the exceptionally high retest reliability of $r = .60$ reported by Kawakami and Dovidio (2001), and exceeds other estimates of $r = .08$ (Bosson et al., 2000) and $r = .13$ (Cunningham et al., 2001). Validity scores of the priming effect lay between those of the EAST and the AAT. Moreover, the priming effect measured during the second test session showed validity coefficients that were nearly as high as the ones of the first priming effect, even though the questionnaires and the BAT were administered during the first session only.

# General Discussion

What do the results reported above tell us about the usefulness of indirect tasks for individual clinical diagnoses, treatment evaluation, and the prediction of relapse? The application of direct tests at an *individual level* requires reliability scores of at least .70 (American Psychological Association, 1954). Bearing that in mind, the EAST and AAT would be considered insufficient for individual application, whereas the APT nearly matches the requirement. Further studies investigating intercorrelations between individual diagnoses based on the APT versus diagnoses based on clinical evaluation will be crucial in defining critical implicit test scores for the conclusion of a diagnosis as well as in the optimization of the task.

However, this critical conclusion regarding the EAST and the AAT may be unfairly premature. First, measuring RTs reliably at the millisecond level is generally very difficult, certainly more difficult than measuring questionnaire responses. Second, the task versions tested here were indirect, that is, the stimulus dimension of interest (whether the pictures showed a spider) was totally irrelevant for the task because participants had to react to head direction of the animals (EAST) or picture format (AAT). Nevertheless, compatibility effects of picture valence and response valence occurred, and most of all, these compatibility effects were related to the individuals' level of spider fear. Thus, even the seemingly low correlations observed here may be considered surprisingly high, and compared to direct measures, the decrease in reliability may be the price one has to pay in return for the increase in resistance to faking attempts (Langner et al., in press). Considering these boundary conditions, the high reliability and validity of the APT are even more impressive.

With regard to validity, it is also doubtful whether one should expect high correlations between indirect tasks and direct measures. On the one hand, one must expect that they are correlated to some degree because in most cases, it is not plausible to assume that implicit fear associations are totally independent of explicit ones. On the other hand, one reason for applying indirect tasks is indeed the assumption that implicit associations are not identical to explicit ones. Thus, in fact they should *not* be highly correlated, even when their reliability would allow for high correlations. This leaves us in the uncomfortable situation that any high or midrange correlation may be taken as evidence for the validity of indirect measures. We therefore consider it crucial to add measures of behavior when determining the validity of indirect tasks. Independently of the strength of the explicit-implicit link, indirect tasks should be able to predict behavior, at least more automatic aspects of it. In this respect, the EAST, AAT, and APT tested here performed fairly well, showing correlations with the BAT between $r = .24$ and $r = .47$.

Regarding the comparative application to different groups, one should not forget that the psychometric properties reported here are based on unselected samples. As long as a task clearly differentiates between high-anxious and low-anxious individuals, it may be a useful tool in the investigation of disorder-specific processing characteristics on a group level. Considering the clear group effects observed earlier (Ellwart et al., 2005; Rinck & Becker, 2007), these tasks might also be applied in the assessment of therapy effects and relapse probability in groups to measure therapeutic change of implicit associations.

Other conclusions from the present study refer to practice effects, that is, whether compatibility effects are reduced with repeated application of the task. This was not the case for the EAST or the APT. In contrast, the AAT reflected an avoidance tendency toward spiders at the first test and a merely neutral tendency at the second test. Therefore, repeated effects measured with the AAT have to be interpreted carefully, considering the participants' previous experience with the task. It also suggests that making indirect tasks like the AAT longer (increasing the number of trials) might not have any beneficial effect on reliability, as it often has with questionnaires. Instead, it may be more relevant to keep the measurement context constant. Research by Ellwart

© 2010 Hogrefe Publishing 

et al. (2005) and others indicates that indirect tasks should be considered measures of the current activation state of implicit associations, not of the mere existence of these associations. Therefore, they should be interpreted as state measures rather than trait measures. This leads to at least two conclusions: First, one cannot expect indirect state measures to show retest reliabilities that are as high as those of questionnaires addressing traits. Second, if one needs high retest reliability of indirect tasks (as in pre-post treatment measurements), one should keep the different test sessions as similar as possible.

Some limitations of the current study need to be highlighted. First, it is important to note that the psychometric properties presented here do not apply to all EASTs, AATs, or APTs in general, but only to the specific versions presented here. Although we tried to design the tasks as similar as possible in terms of materials, participants, and duration, we cannot conclude that the APT is generally superior to the EAST and the AAT. In fact, a controlled variation of temporal parameters (e.g., presentation times), materials (e.g., stimuli more perfectly tailored to the individual fears such as small vs. large spiders), and symptom activation (e.g., presence of a real threat object during the tasks) might lead to an optimized version with satisfying psychometric quality for each of the tasks. Moreover, the reported properties apply only to the specific samples of participants described here, that is, unselected groups of students. One may expect the psychometric properties to improve in extreme groups.

To summarize, the present paper adds to the current literature on the psychometric quality of indirect tasks and their suitability as assessment instruments in individual diagnostics. Our study provides comparative results on psychometric properties for three different indirect tasks, using similar materials and populations, and tapping into the same clinical construct. Although very useful in group comparisons, most of the indirect tasks do not seem suitable yet for reliable individual assessment. However, the results of this study encourage the application of indirect tasks in clinical contexts as well as the optimization of the tasks for individual use. Currently, they are helpful diagnostic tools to be used in addition to, rather than instead of, direct measures.

## Acknowledgments

Preparation of this paper was supported by a grant from the German Research Foundation (DFG) to Eni Becker and Mike Rinck. We are very grateful to Kristin Grundl and Kira Marschner who helped in recruiting and testing the participants.

# References

American Psychological Association. (1954). *Technical recommendations for psychological tests and diagnostic techniques*. Washington, DC: APA.

Banse, R. (1999). Automatic evaluation of self and significant others: Affective Priming in close relationships. *Journal of Social and Personal Relationships, 16*, 803–821.

Beck, A. T., Emery, G., & Greenberg, R. (1985). *Anxiety disorders and phobias: A cognitive perspective*. New York: Basic Books.

Birch, C. D., Stewart, S. H., Wiers, R. W., Klein, R. M., MacLean, A. D., & Berish, M. J. (2008). The mood-induced activation of implicit alcohol cognition in enhancement and coping motivated drinkers. *Addictive Behaviors, 33*, 565–581.

Bosson, J. K., Swann, W. B. Jr., & Pennebaker, J. W. (2000). Stalking the perfect measure of implicit self-esteem: The blind men and the elephant revisited? *Journal of Personality and Social Psychology, 79*, 631–643.

Chambless, D. L., Caputo, G. C., Bright, P., & Gallagher, R. (1984). Assessment of fear of fear in agoraphobics: The body sensations questionnaire and the agoraphobic cognitions questionnaire. *Journal of Consulting and Clinical Psychology, 52*, 1090–1097.

Coles, M. E., & Heimberg, R. G. (2002). Memory biases in the anxiety disorders: Current status. *Clinical Psychology Review, 22*, 587–627.

Cunningham, W. A., Preacher, K. J., & Banaji, M. R. (2001). Implicit attitude measures: Consistency, stability, and convergent validity. *Psychological Science, 12*, 163–170.

De Houwer, J. (2003). The Extrinsic Affective Simon Task. *Experimental Psychology, 50*, 77–85.

De Houwer, J., & de Bruycker, E. (2007). The implicit association test outperforms the Extrinsic Affective Simon Task as an implicit measure of inter-individual differences in attitudes. *British Journal of Social Psychology, 46*, 401–421.

De Houwer, J., Hermans, D., Rothermund, K., & Wentura, D. (2002). Affective priming of semantic categorization responses. *Cognition and Emotion, 16*, 643–666.

De Jong, P. J., Pasman, W., Kindt, M., & van den Hout, M. A. (2001). A reaction time paradigm to assess (implicit) complaint-specific dysfunctional beliefs. *Behaviour Research and Therapy, 39*, 101–113.

De Jong, P. J., Wiers, R. W., van de Braak, M., & Huijding, J. (2007). Using the extrinsic affective Simon test as a measure of implicit attitudes towards alcohol: Relationship with drinking behaviour and alcohol problems. *Addictive Behavior, 32*, 881–887.

Ehlers, A., Margraf, J., & Chambless, D. L. (1993). *Fragebogen zu körperbezogenen Ängsten, Kognitionen und Vermeidung (AKV)*. Weinheim: Beltz.

Ellwart, T., Becker, E. S., & Rinck, M. (2005). Activation and measurement of threat associations in fear of spiders: An application of the Extrinsic Affective Simon Task. *Journal of Behaviour Therapy and Experimental Psychiatry, 36*, 281–299.

Ellwart, T., Rinck, M., & Becker, E. (2006). From fear to love: Implicit and explicit associations towards spiders. *Emotion, 6*, 18–27.

Fazio, R. H., Sanbonmatsu, D., Powell, M., & Kardes, F. (1986). On the automatic activation of attitudes. *Journal of Personality and Social Psychology, 50*, 229–238.

Huijding, J., & de Jong, P. (2005). A pictorial version of the Extrinsic Affective Simon Task: Sensitivity to generally affective and phobia-relevant stimuli in high and low spider fearful individuals. *Experimental Psychology, 52*, 289–295.

Huijding, J., & de Jong, P. (2009). Implicit and explicit attitudes toward spiders: Sensitivity to treatment and predictive value for generalization of treatment effects. *Cognitive Therapy and Research, 33*, 211–220.

Kawakami, K., & Dovidio, J. F. (2001). The reliability of implicit stereotyping. *Personality and Social Psychology Bulletin, 27*, 212–225.

 © 2010 Hogrefe Publishing

Kuehner, C. (1997). *Fragebogen zur Depressionsdiagnostik nach DSM-IV (FDD-DSM-IV)*. Göttingen, Germany: Hogrefe.

Langner, O., Ouwens, M., Muskens, M., Trumpf, J., Becker, E. S., & Rinck, M. (in press). Faking on direct, indirect, and behavioural measures of spider fear: Can you get away with it? *Cognition and Emotion*.

Laux, L., Glanzmann, P., Schaffner, P., & Spielberger, C. D. (1981). *STAI: Das State-Trait-Angstinventar*. Weinheim, Germany: Beltz.

LeDoux, J. (1996). *The emotional brain*. New York: Simon & Schuster.

Mathews, A., & MacLeod, C. (2005). Cognitive vulnerability to emotional disorders. *Annual Review of Clinical Psychology, 1*, 167–195.

Öhman, A. (1993). Fear and anxiety as emotional phenomena. In M. Lewis & J. Haviland (Eds.), *Handbook of emotions*. New York: Guilford Press.

Reinecke, A., Rinck, M., & Becker, E. S. (2006). Spiders crawl easily through the bottleneck: Visual working memory for negative stimuli. *Emotion, 6*, 438–449.

Reinecke, A., Rinck, M., & Becker, E. S. (2008). How preferential is the preferential encoding of threatening stimuli? Working memory biases in specific anxiety and the attentional blink. *Journal of Anxiety Disorders, 22*, 655–670.

Rinck, M., & Becker, E. S. (2007). Approach and avoidance in fear of spiders. *Journal of Behaviour Therapy and Experimental Psychiatry, 38*, 105–120.

Rinck, M., Bundschuh, S., Engler, S., Müller, A., Wissmann, J., Ellwart, T., & Becker, E. S. (2002). Reliability and validity of German versions of three instruments measuring fear of spiders. *Diagnostica, 48*, 141–149.

Szymanski, J., & O'Donohue, W. (1995). Fear of spiders questionnaire. *Journal of Behavior Therapy and Experimental Psychiatry, 26*, 31–34.

Teachman, B. A., & Woody, S. R. (2003). Automatic processing in spider phobia: Implicit fear associations over the course of treatment. *Journal of Abnormal Psychology, 112*, 100–109.

Teige, S., Schnabel, K., Banse, R., & Asendorpf, J. B. (2004). Assessment of multiple implicit self-concept dimensions using the Extrinsic Affective Simon Task (EAST). *European Journal of Personality, 18*, 495–520.

Zimmermann, M., Coryell, W., Wilson, S., & Corenthal, C. (1986). A self-report scale to diagnose major depressive disorder. *Archives of General Psychiatry, 43*, 1076–1081.

Andrea Reinecke

Department of Psychiatry
University of Oxford
Warneford Hospital
Warneford Lane
Headington
Oxford
OX3 7JX
UK
Tel. + 44 1865 226471
E-mail andrea.reinecke@psych.ox.ac.uk

© 2010 Hogrefe Publishing 

Original Article

# Easier When Done Than Said!

## Implicit Self-Esteem Predicts Observed or Spontaneous Behavior, but Not Self-Reported or Controlled Behavior

Almut Rudolph,[1] Michela Schröder-Abé,[1] Michael Riketta,[†,2] and Astrid Schütz[1]

[1]Chemnitz University of Technology, Germany
[2]University of Tübingen, Germany

**Abstract.** Evidence for the criterion validity of indirect self-esteem measures is still limited, with only some studies finding effects of implicit (ISE) independent of explicit (ESE) self-esteem. This may be due to the fact that studies predicting actual behavior are particularly rare. The present study contributes evidence to the predictive validity of the Implicit Association Test and a recently developed self-judgment task under cognitive load. We used criteria beyond self-report: experimenter ratings of anxiety, linguistic aspects of anxiety, and spontaneous self-confident behaviors. Using paired criteria, we tested a double dissociation of ISE and ESE. Results supported our hypothesis: ISE predicted self-confident behaviors or aspects of anxiety that ESE was not able to predict, and vice versa. Thus, differential predictive validity of both measures of self-esteem was demonstrated. With behavioral criteria that tapped into impulsive processes, ISE was a better predictor than ESE was.

**Keywords:** implicit self-esteem, explicit self-esteem, Implicit Association Test, behavior prediction, LIWC

In the past 12 years, research on implicit self-esteem (ISE) has been prominent in social and personality psychology. But only few studies have found evidence for criterion validity in measures of ISE (Conner & Barrett, 2005; Spalding & Hardin, 1999): ISE rarely produced main effects independent of explicit self-esteem (ESE). How can this be explained, given the fact that evidence for reliability and construct validity of several indirect measures has been established (e.g., Bosson, Swann, & Pennebaker, 2000; Rudolph, Schröder-Abé, Schütz, Gregg, & Sedikides, 2008)? In contrast to evidence in the field of ISE, incremental validity of indirect measures over and above direct measures has already been demonstrated in other domains, such as anxiety or shyness (Asendorpf, Banse, & Mücke, 2002; Egloff & Schmukle, 2002). A closer look at those studies reveals that behavioral outcomes (instead of mere self-report) have been used as criteria. In the present article, we therefore used observer ratings to examine the predictive validity of indirect measures of self-esteem. In line with a dual-process approach (Strack & Deutsch, 2004), we further argue that it is essential to use observed and spontaneous behaviors when the goal is to evaluate the criterion validity in measures of ISE.

Dual-process approaches provide an elaborate framework of ISE and ESE. These models presume two structurally distinct, albeit interrelated, systems of information processing: an *impulsive system* that processes information automatically and in an associative format, and a *reflective system* that processes information deliberately and in a propositional format (e.g., Strack & Deutsch, 2004). ESE is the "positivity of a person's evaluation of the self" (Baumeister, 1998) that is consciously accessible and mentally represented in a propositional format in the reflective system. ESE is overtly expressed in self-reports and measured on the basis of direct measures such as questionnaires. ISE is an individual's overlearned, automatic, and not necessarily conscious self-evaluation (Greenwald & Farnham, 2000). It is represented in the associative network of the impulsive system and can be assessed with indirect measures such as the Implicit Association Test (IAT; Greenwald & Farnham, 2000). Indirect measures of self-esteem seek to infer people's attitudes toward themselves from their reactions to stimuli representing the self (e.g., first person pronouns), typically under conditions in which people are either unaware of or lack control over the measurement process (De Houwer, 2006).

Dual-process approaches specify how behavioral schemata are activated by input from the reflective and impulsive system (Strack & Deutsch, 2004). In the reflective system, a behavioral option is weighted and integrated by the value and the probability of its potential consequences. In the impulsive system, behavioral schemata are triggered through spreading activation in the associative store without the need of deliberation and introspection.

In line with the preceding explanation, direct and indirect measures assess self-evaluations within the two information processing systems, and thus differentially predict behaviors. Direct measures tap into propositional representations and should be more strongly related to consciously controlled behaviors (e.g., self-reports and controlled observable behaviors), as those behaviors are activated deliberately and based on introspection. Indirect measures should have a


DOI: 10.1027/0044-3409/a000003
© 2010 Hogrefe Publishing

stronger link to automatic and spontaneous behaviors because indirect measures tap into associative structures. In addition, indirect measures should be useful in predicting aspects of personality and behavior that are less subject to deliberative control than others. Such aspects of personality and behavior can be assessed by observers who are assumed to have better information about a person's appearance from the "outside" than does the person him- or herself (Vazire & Mehl, 2008). In detail, when asked for an overall impression of a specific aspect of personality, observers will focus more strongly on spontaneous behaviors to reveal the true feeling or attitude of a person and less strongly on controlled behavior, as the latter is more easily influenced by impression management efforts (DePaulo, 1992). Along these lines, promising results have been shown with respect to implicit self-concept aspects such as anxiety, neuroticism, extraversion, agreeableness, and conscientiousness (Egloff & Schmukle, 2002; Steffens & Schulze König, 2006). One study has in fact demonstrated a *double dissociation* for the construct of shyness: Direct measures predicted controlled shy behavior that indirect measures were not able to predict whereas indirect measures predicted spontaneous shy behavior that direct measures were not able to predict (Asendorpf et al., 2002).

Despite those encouraging results from other personality domains, only very few studies found significant main effects of ISE. This may be due to the fact that studies predicting criteria beyond self-report are particularly rare in the field of self-esteem. Based on the theoretical considerations, criteria should be chosen that can hardly be controlled or do not require deliberation. The lack of correspondence between indirect measures and appropriate criteria may have been responsible for the absence of convincing evidence of criterion validity in measures of ISE.

Two studies that found main effects of ISE did indeed use criteria beyond self-report: Conner and Barrett (2005) used an experience sampling procedure of emotional experiences, and Spalding and Hardin (1999) used interviewers' ratings of participants' anxiety. Actual behavior was only used in the latter study. That study, however, is not perfectly conclusive as ISE was measured with a priming task (e.g., Fazio, Jackson, Dunton, & Williams, 1995). Although priming tasks sometimes are used in the assessment of ISE, their reliability has been shown to be low (Bosson et al., 2000). In addition, the fact that the finding has not been replicated or extended for a whole decade raises the question whether it can be relied upon.

Based on the arguments elaborated above, we focused on observable and spontaneous behavioral criteria to test the criterion validity of ISE measures. Specifically, we concentrated on behaviors that participants are hardly able to control or that they do not try to control. As little is known about the behavioral correlates of self-esteem, choosing the criteria to validate measures of ISE is not a trifle. The effects of self-esteem are especially pronounced in self-relevant situations such as work performance and interpersonal relations where they are assumed to stimulate self-regulative processes. Empirically, ESE has been shown to predict behaviors such as assertiveness and confidence: People with high self-esteem are more outgoing, assertive, confident, and less anxious than others (Leary & MacDonald, 2003). Thus, we used anxiousness (Study 1) and nonverbally expressed self-confidence (Study 2) as criteria. To measure spontaneous and less controlled aspects of behavior, we took into account the following aspects. First, we employed word use as an objective behavioral indicator (Fast & Funder, 2008). Word use and directly observed behavior have been shown to be strongly related in laboratory and real life settings (Fast & Funder, 2008), and word use is a more indirect and thus less controllable measure than asking participants for direct self-reports of the trait or behavior of interest. Second, we used experimenter and independent observer ratings instead of self-reported behavior, as observers form their judgment in large parts on the basis of cues such as spontaneous body movements beyond the actor's control (DePaulo, 1992). Finally, to directly compare the results for controlled and spontaneous behavior we conducted a fine-grained analysis of videotaped nonverbal behavior (Study 2). We hypothesized that there would be a double dissociation of ISE and ESE. Specifically, we expected that ISE alone should predict spontaneous aspects of self-confident behavior that ESE is not able to predict and ESE should predict controlled aspects of self-confident behaviors that ISE is not able to predict.

## Study 1

Study 1 aimed at a conceptual replication and extension of previous research on the prediction of behavior with ISE. Spalding and Hardin (1999) had shown that ISE predicted experimenter ratings of anxiety. That study was extended in two ways. First, we used a different measure of ISE, the newly developed and validated LOAD task (Riketta & Gebauer, 2009). The LOAD task is an ISE measure in which participants respond to self-descriptive items under conditions of cognitive load. It is considered an indirect measure insofar as the cognitive load taxes participants' cognitive resources and inhibits deliberative self-reflection and impression management (Riketta & Gebauer, 2009). Second, we not only used experimenter ratings of anxiety during a self-relevant interview, but in addition analyzed word use as a linguistic indicator of anxiety.

In detail, participants completed a writing task and an interview. Nonself-reported anxiety was inferred from the usage of anxiousness-related words in a writing task and experimenter ratings of anxiety during a self-relevant interview. In addition, self-reported nervousness and state anxiety were assessed. Assuming a double dissociation, we hypothesized that ESE, but not ISE, would predict self-reported nervousness and anxiety, whereas ISE, but not ESE, would predict linguistic aspects of anxiety and experimenter-rated anxiety.

### Method

#### Participants and Procedure

A total of 79 students (62 female, $M_{age}$ = 23.2, $SD$ = 5.2) participated. Individually, participants first completed measures of ISE and ESE as well as a measure of nervousness.

© 2010 Hogrefe Publishing 

Then they completed a writing task in which they briefly introduced themselves in 10 sentences. Then, a self-relevant interview was conducted. The experimenter asked the participants to describe their strengths and weaknesses, and to remember and describe examples of a social situation in which participants had been rejected and then to answer questions about that situation (e.g., How did you feel?). After that interview participants rated their anxiety during the interview and the experimenter also rated the participant's apparent anxiety. Finally, participants were thanked and fully debriefed.

## Measures

### ISE

The self-judgment task under cognitive load (LOAD; Riketta & Gebauer, 2009) was used to assess self-esteem indirectly. After three practice trials, 15 positive (e.g., creative and thoughtful) and 15 negative (e.g., immature and careless) self-trait words were presented in random order. Participants were asked to press one of two response keys to indicate whether a trait described them or not. The words remained on the screen until the participant responded. To ensure spontaneous responding, cognitive load was established by asking participants to memorize an eight-digit number, rehearse it during the task, and re-enter it at the end of the task. Eighty-five percent of participants entered the right number and the remaining participants had only minor errors (such as transposed digits), so all participants were retained in further analyses. ISE scores were computed by subtracting the number of negative traits endorsed from the number of positive traits endorsed. Higher LOAD scores reflect higher ISE.

### ESE

The 32-item Multidimensional Self-Esteem Scale (MSES; Schütz & Sellin, 2006) was used to measure ESE (e.g., "Do you doubt yourself?" or "How often do you think that you are useless?"). Responses were made on 7-point scales with end points labeled *not at all* (1) and *very much* (7) or *never* (1) and *always* (7), respectively.

### Nervousness

Nervousness was measured with the respective subscale of the Trier Personality Inventory (Becker, 1989). Items (e.g., "I ... feel my heart beating fast and irregularly") were answered on a 4-point scale (1 = *always*, 4 = *never*). To obtain comparability with the measures used in this study, answers were inverted so that high scores represent the tendency to be anxious.

### Linguistic Aspects of Anxiety

Linguistic indicators of anxiety were derived from the writing task. Participants wrote about themselves but were not directly asked to report about anxiety. Instead, word use served as an indirect measure of anxiety. We used the linguistic inquiry and word count (LIWC; Pennebaker, Francis, & Booth, 2001; German version by Wolf et al., 2008) to determine the frequency with which participants used anxiety-related words (e.g., nervous and afraid). The score expressed the proportion of words that fell into the anxiety category of the LIWC.

### Self- and Experimenter-Rated Anxiety During Interview

Self-ratings of how anxious participants felt during the interview were assessed with a 10-item scale (e.g., anxious and tense). Experimenter ratings were calculated as the mean of a 2-item scale (anxious, nervous) on which the experimenter, who was unaware of the participants' self-esteem scores, rated the overall impression of participants' apparent anxiety. All ratings were administered on 7-point scales (1 = *not at all* and 7 = *very much*).

## Results and Discussion

Table 1 shows the descriptive statistics and correlations of the main variables. All measures had satisfactory to high reliabilities. Further, ISE and ESE were not significantly correlated, albeit the correlation was somewhat higher than in previous studies. ESE was significantly correlated with self-rated anxiety and nervousness but not with experimenter-rated and LIWC anxiety. ISE did not correlate with self-rated anxiety and nervousness but significantly with experimenter-rated and marginally significantly with LIWC anxiety.

In a path model, we tested the double dissociation pattern (see Figure 1, upper part). MSES and LOAD scores were entered as exogenous variables, self-rated anxiety and nervousness as well as experimenter-rated anxiety and LIWC anxiety were entered as endogenous variables. Causal paths from the MSES to self-rated anxiety and nervousness, and from the LOAD task to experimenter-rated anxiety and LIWC anxiety were included. In addition to the predictive relations between self-esteem and criterion measures, we analyzed the overall fit of the model.

As can be seen in the upper part of Figure 1, the MSES significantly predicted self-rated anxiety and nervousness, whereas the LOAD task significantly predicted experimenter-rated anxiety and LIWC anxiety, with the latter coefficient being only marginally significant. Moreover, the specified model was confirmed as indicated by good fit indices: $\chi^2(11) = 7.99$, $p = .71$, $\chi^2/df = 0.73$, RMSEA = 0.00, SRMR = 0.08, CFI = 1.00, and GFI = 0.97.

We also tested a less restricted model with paths from the MSES to experimenter-rated and LIWC anxiety, paths from the LOAD task to self-rated anxiety and nervousness, and correlated exogenous variables (see Figure 1, upper part, dashed paths). Those paths as well as a chi-square difference test were not significant ($\chi^2_D(5) = 2.80$, $p > .05$). Therefore, we assume an identical fit of the models and prefer the


© 2010 Hogrefe Publishing

*Table 1.* Descriptive statistics and correlations between indices of self-esteem and criteria

| Measures | Min | Max | *M* | *SD* | $\alpha^a$ | 1 | 2 | 3 | 4 | 5 |
|---|---|---|---|---|---|---|---|---|---|---|
| *Study 1* | | | | | | | | | | |
| 1. MSES | 2.41 | 6.25 | 4.24 | 0.97 | .93 | – | | | | |
| 2. LOAD | −8 | 15 | 8.58 | 4.04 | .73 | .12 | – | | | |
| 3. Self-rated anxiety | 1.00 | 6.10 | 2.53 | 1.05 | .89 | −.23* | −.07 | – | | |
| 4. Self-rated nervousness | 1.09 | 3.82 | 2.54 | 0.85 | .95 | −.74** | −.12 | .26* | – | |
| 5. Experimenter-rated anxiety | 1.00 | 5.50 | 1.87 | 1.23 | .79 | −.13 | −.22* | .14 | .18 | – |
| 6. LIWC anxiety | 0.00 | 4.76 | 0.49 | 1.03 | na | −.09 | −.19[†] | .05 | .16 | −.02 |
| *Study 2* | | | | | | | | | | |
| 1. MSES | 2.94 | 6.28 | 4.88 | 0.72 | .92 | – | | | | |
| 2. IAT | −0.08 | 1.22 | 0.83 | 0.30 | .78 | −.07 | – | | | |
| 3. Controlled behavior[b] | 1.21 | 2.86 | 2.01 | 0.40 | .72 | .35* | .15 | – | | |
| 4. Spontaneous behavior[b] | 1.00 | 2.80 | 1.85 | 0.40 | .82 | −.08 | .29* | −.05 | – | |

*Note.* $N_{\text{Study 1}} = 79$, $N_{\text{Study 2}} = 49$. MSES = Multidimensional Self-Esteem Scale, LOAD = self-judgment task under cognitive load, IAT = Implicit Association Test, LIWC = linguistic inquiry and word count.
[a]Internal consistency for self-esteem measures and anxiety ratings; Interrater agreement between two observer judgments of behavioral ratings using independent ratings of 15% randomly selected participants.
[b]Average rating of behavioral ratings: Higher scores indicate more self-confident controlled and spontaneous behavior (i.e., more illustrators and less adaptors).
$^{\dagger}p < .10$, $^{*}p < .05$, $^{**}p < .01$.

simpler model according to the parsimony principle (Kline, 2005).

In sum, the hypothesized double dissociation pattern of ESE and ISE was clearly confirmed in a path model. ISE predicted the use of anxiety-related words in a writing task and experimenter-rated anxiety during an interview but not self-rated anxiety and nervousness. Furthermore, ESE predicted self-rated anxiety and nervousness but not experimenter-rated or LIWC anxiety.

The results of this initial study were the first to replicate Spalding and Hardin (1999), thereby extending the findings by using a recently developed measure of ISE, the LOAD task, and by using an additional unobtrusive measure of anxiety that is based on word use. To sum up, ISE predicted nonself-report criteria (i.e., observer judgments and word use) that can be considered indirect indicators of self-confidence.

## Study 2

Study 1 relied on experimenter ratings to assess anxiety. We reasoned that the experimenter would at least in part use indicators beyond the participant's control to make this judgment, as previous research has shown that observers tend to rely on spontaneous behaviors when looking for indicators that cannot be faked (DePaulo, 1992). In Study 2 we followed up on that and aimed at more closely differentiating controlled and spontaneous behavioral indicators to investigate whether these indicators would be differentially predicted by ISE and ESE.

For this purpose, we employed a rather fine-grained nonverbal behavioral analysis of controlled versus spontaneous indicators of self-confidence during a presentation task. Most importantly, we distinguished between adaptors and illustrators, which are two types of nonverbal behaviors that vary with respect to the required level of control (Ekman & Friesen, 1969). Whereas *adaptors* are unintentional gestures that are used spontaneously and less consciously, *illustrators* are intentionally used hand movements that underline spoken words (Ekman & Friesen, 1969). Adaptors are assumed to be triggered by behavioral schemata which in turn are directly activated through spreading activation in the impulsive system, whereas illustrators can be viewed as "reasoned action" that is influenced by intentional and rational processes in the reflective system (Strack & Deutsch, 2004). Previous research has shown that direct measures of shyness are related to illustrators and indirect measures of shyness are related to adaptors and that illustrators are indeed more controllable than adaptors (Asendorpf et al., 2002).

Furthermore, our investigation had yet to include the most promising and most widely used methodology, the IAT (see De Houwer, 2006). The IAT was found to be a reliable measure of ISE (Rudolph et al., 2008) and was successfully validated when measuring anxiety and shyness (Asendorpf et al., 2002; Egloff & Schmukle, 2002).

We extended Study 1 in various ways. First, we tested predictive validity of ISE and ESE, and assessed the criteria 1 week after the predictors. Second, behavioral criteria were not rated by the experimenter during the experimental situation but systematically categorized by independent observers who watched videotaped sequences. Most importantly, we were able to differentiate controlled and spontaneous aspects of behavior to investigate whether these would be differentially predicted by ESE and ISE. As in Study 1, we hypothesized a double dissociation pattern and predicted that ISE would predict spontaneous behaviors better than ESE, whereas ESE would predict controlled behavior better than ISE.

© 2010 Hogrefe Publishing

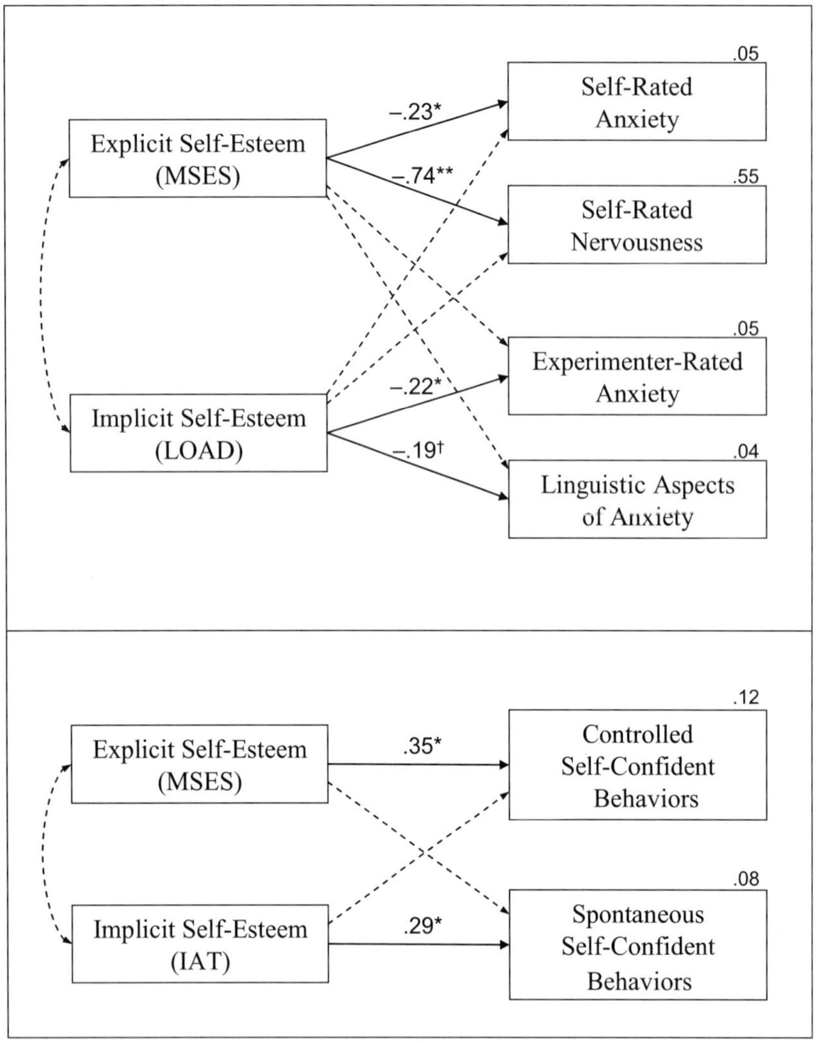


*Figure 1.* The path models illustrate the double dissociation pattern between explicit and implicit self-esteem (including standardized beta weights and variance estimates) in Study 1 (upper part) and Study 2 (lower part). Dashed lines represent removed non-significant causal and correlation paths: $^{\dagger}p < .10$, $^{*}p < .05$, $^{**}p < .01$.

## Method

### Participants and Procedure

A total of 49 students (37 female, $M_{age} = 22.8$, $SD = 4.3$) signed up for two sessions in the laboratory. In the first session, groups of up to three participants completed measures of ISE and ESE. Exactly 1 week later, participants individually attended a second session during which they were videotaped. They received instructions for a public speaking task that was adopted from Egloff and Schmukle (2002). Participants were asked to give a 3-min oral presentation on a scientific text. The instructor emphasized that the ability to comprehend and present scientific issues under time pressure is an important ability in successfully completing academic studies. Participants were told that they had 10 min to prepare a speech that would later be scored by a panel of judges who would rate their level of competence. After completing the presentation, participants were debriefed in detail. They were informed that the study was not designed to measure their ability and that the videotapes would only be viewed by trained raters for scientific purposes.

### Measures

#### ISE

Participants completed the generic affective variant of the self-esteem IAT (Greenwald & Farnham, 2000) in which participants were asked to coclassify self-related and self-unrelated stimuli (e.g., self, my; others, yours) alongside positive and negative stimuli (e.g., smile, joy; pain, war). We used the same structure and scoring procedure as in Rudolph et al. (2008). Higher IAT scores reflect higher ISE.

#### ESE

As in Study 1, ESE was measured with the MSES (Schütz & Sellin, 2006).

#### Controlled and Spontaneous Self-Confident Behaviors

Measures of controlled and spontaneous self-confident behaviors were rated by a trained observer who was unaware of participants' ISE and ESE. A category system distinguished different types of spontaneous and controlled nonverbal behaviors (Ekman & Friesen, 1969). The ratings were provided separately on 4-point scales (1 = *not at all* and 4 = *very often*) in each category: facial adaptors (nervous mouth movements, e.g., lip biting or licking and pressing the lips together), body adaptors (nervous hand movements, e.g., rubbing or squeezing fore arm or upper arm and playing with one's fingers), illustrators (hand movements, e.g., emphasizing a particular phrase and sketching the direction of ones thoughts), and control of posture and control of speech (perceived control of posture and speech on 4-point scales, 1 = *very tense* or *dysfluent* and 4 = very *relaxed* or *fluent*). Ratings of illustrators, control of posture and speech were aggregated into a mean rating of controlled behavior. High scores indicate a high level of *controlled self-confident behaviors*. Adaptors were reverse coded and aggregated into a mean rating of *spontaneous self-confident behaviors*. Higher scores reflect a higher level of self-confident spontaneous behaviors (i.e., less frequent use of adaptors during the speech). To ensure rating reliability, a random subsample comprising 15% of the videos was additionally rated by a second independent observer and interrater agreement was calculated.

### Results and Discussion

The bottom section of Table 1 shows the descriptive statistics and correlations. The MSES was highly reliable, the reliability of the IAT and the interrater agreement of the behavior ratings were satisfactory. Again, ISE and ESE were uncorrelated. Also controlled and spontaneous self-confident behaviors were not correlated.

In order to test our hypothesized double dissociation pattern, we employed path modeling (see Figure 1, lower part). The exogenous variables MSES and IAT were related to the endogenous variables of controlled and spontaneous self-confident behavior, respectively. The MSES significantly predicted controlled self-confident behavior and the IAT significantly predicted spontaneous self-confident behavior. The model constituted a good fit: $\chi^2(4) = 2.43$, $p = .66$; $\chi^2/df = 0.61$, RMSEA = 0.00, SRMR = 0.06, CFI = 1.00, and GFI = 0.98.

Additionally, a less restricted model with paths from the MSES to spontaneous behavior, from the IAT to controlled behavior and correlated exogenous variables was tested (see Figure 1, lower part, dashed paths). The added paths were not statistically significant, however, and with a nonsignificant chi-square difference test ($\chi^2_D$ (3) = 2.05, $p > .05$), we assume an identical fit of both models. Based on the parsimony principle, we prefer the simpler model (Kline, 2005).

Overall, the pattern replicated the results of Study 1 and established predictive validity for direct and indirect measures of self-esteem. The direct measure of self-esteem predicted controlled indicators of self-confident behaviors while the indirect measure of self-esteem did not. The indirect measure of self-esteem predicted spontaneous indicators of self-confident behaviors while the direct measure of self-esteem did not. Most importantly, this study replicated a double dissociation of ISE and ESE using another indirect measure of self-esteem – the IAT – and more fine-grained independent observer ratings of self-confident behaviors.

## General Discussion

The present study is one of the first to provide compelling evidence for the criterion validity of indirect measures of self-esteem. Across two studies and three sets of dependent variables, measures of ISE (the LOAD task and the IAT) that tap into spontaneous and automatic self-evaluations predicted self-confident behaviors (either rated by an experimenter or by an observer or as reflected in word usage) that the measure of ESE was not able to predict. By contrast, measures of ESE that rely on self-reports of participants' explicit attitudes toward the self predicted controlled and deliberative behaviors that measures of ISE were not able to predict. In accordance with dual-process approaches, the data support the hypothesized double dissociation pattern between ISE and ESE.

The present study contributes to the existing literature in several ways. First, we provided converging evidence for the criterion validity of ISE measures. This is remarkable since results showing significant main effects of ISE had been rare after the initial study by Spalding and Hardin (1999). In the present research, two different measures of ISE were shown to produce independent effects in predicting observed behavior. Using indicators of self-confidence that tap into impulsive processes, we found replicable evidence of the predictive validity of ISE. Thus, we consider it safe to assume that ISE measures are valid, but a lack of correspondence between measures and criteria has precluded evidence of criterion validity in previous research.

Second, our findings support the differential predictive validity of ISE and ESE in a double dissociation pattern. More precisely, ESE was uniquely related to self-reported and controlled nonverbal indicators of self-confident behavior, whereas ISE was uniquely related to observed, indirectly assessed, and spontaneous nonverbal indicators of self-confidence. There were significant relations neither between ESE and observed or spontaneous self-confident behaviors nor between ISE and self-reported or controlled self-confident behaviors. Our results provide evidence for the theoretical framework that direct and indirect measures of self-esteem tap into distinct systems of information processing, and therefore differentially predict behaviors.

Third, our results once again demonstrate that questionnaire ratings should be complemented by observer ratings of personality and observations of actual behavior. As expected, ISE predicted observer-rated anxiety and spontaneous behavior. Correlations were slightly above |.30| which is as high as the typical coefficient that has been found for the relation between behavior and self-reports (Mischel, 1968). Overall, there are only few studies available that show the prediction of behavior on the basis of personality traits. Thus, our research responds to recent calls for a broader range of data in personality psychology (Funder, 2001) and for using behavioral data (Baumeister, Vohs, &

© 2010 Hogrefe Publishing

Funder, 2007). In doing so, we extend previous research by focusing on indirect measures and ISE.

Finally, the present research provides evidence on the usefulness of the indirect assessment of self-esteem in the study of human behavior: By predicting behavior that ESE was not able to predict, we extend findings on the well-established *construct* of self-esteem. For a thorough understanding of self-esteem processes, ISE apparently is a very important complement to ESE (see also Schröder-Abé, Rudolph, & Schütz, 2007; Schröder-Abé, Rudolph, Wiesner, & Schütz, 2007).

Despite the interesting and consistent results, the present study has some limitations. First, in both studies, data were gathered during laboratory observations and it is not clear how they generalize to everyday settings. In weighing pros and cons, we preferred this approach to benefit from standardized setting (Lakes & Hoyt, 2008). Being aware of this constraint, we used different sources of ratings (overall impressions of experimenters who were present in the situation versus more fine-grained independent observer ratings) and different situations (a self-relevant interview vs. a scientific presentation) in the two studies to generalize the results beyond one specific design. As some of the behaviors we assessed (e.g., illustrators) may not be consistent between one type of situation (e.g., giving a talk) and another (e.g., first date), it would still be interesting to see whether our results are replicable in differently framed laboratory settings, in everyday settings, and with acquaintances' ratings of behavior.

Because of lengthy experimental sessions and laborious behavior coding, the second limitation of the present study is its sample size which may be considered as small for path modeling. However, in spite of limited statistical power in small samples, we replicated our results across two studies.

Our findings also provide some directions for future research. As has been shown by Friese, Hofmann, and Schmitt (2008), the predictive validity of indirect measures is typically high when there is little opportunity or motivation to control behavior. Similarly there should be conditions under which the predictive validity of direct measures is higher or lower. We differentiated between aspects of behavior that vary with respect to controllability (e.g., illustrators and adaptors) and found differential criterion validity. We did not manipulate behavioral control, however. Future research should include conditions that vary with respect to such aspects.

Clearly, after a decade of research on measures of ISE, a lot of questions have not yet been answered. But the results of this study help to provide evidence on the predictive validity of those measures. We used theoretically and empirically derived behavioral indicators. Constituting a double dissociation pattern, direct and indirect measures of self-esteem differentially predicted those indicators. In order to predict behavior over and above the effects of ESE, it seems therefore essential to consider ISE in future studies.

## Acknowledgment

The research was supported by the German Research Foundation (Grant SCHU 1459/2).

## References

Asendorpf, J. B., Banse, R., & Mücke, D. (2002). Double dissociation between implicit and explicit personality self-concept: The case of shy behavior. *Journal of Personality and Social Psychology, 83*, 380–393.

Baumeister, R. F. (1998). The self. In D. T. Gilbert, S. T. Fiske, & G. Lindzey (Eds.), *The handbook of social psychology* (Vol. 1). New York: McGraw-Hill.

Baumeister, R. F., Vohs, K. D., & Funder, D. C. (2007). Psychology as the science of self-reports and finger-movements. Whatever happened to actual behavior? *Perspectives on Psychological Science, 2*, 396–403.

Becker, P. (1989). Trierer Persönlichkeitsfragebogen (TPF) [Trier personality inventory]. Göttingen: Hogrefe.

Bosson, J. K., Swann, W. B. J., & Pennebaker, J. W. (2000). Stalking the perfect measure of implicit self-esteem: The blind men and the elephant revisited? *Journal of Personality and Social Psychology, 79*, 631–643.

Conner, T., & Barrett, L. F. (2005). Implicit self-attitudes predict spontaneous affect in daily life. *Emotion, 5*, 476–488.

De Houwer, J. (2006). What are implicit measures and why are we using them? In R. W. J. Wiers & A. W. Stacy (Eds.), *Handbook of implicit cognition and addiction* (pp. 11–28). Thousand Oaks, CA: Sage.

DePaulo, B. M. (1992). Nonverbal behavior and self-presentation. *Psychological Bulletin, 111*, 203–243.

Egloff, B., & Schmukle, S. C. (2002). Predictive validity of an Implicit Association Test for assessing anxiety. *Journal of Personality and Social Psychology, 83*, 1441–1455.

Ekman, P., & Friesen, W. V. (1969). The repertoire of nonverbal behavior: Categories, origins, usage and coding. *Semiotica, 1*, 49–98.

Fast, L. A., & Funder, D. C. (2008). Personality as manifest in word use: Correlations with self-report, acquaintance report, and behavior. *Journal of Personality and Social Psychology, 94*, 334–346.

Fazio, R. H., Jackson, J. R., Dunton, B. C., & Williams, C. J. (1995). Variability in automatic activation as an unobtrusive measure of racial attitudes: A bona fide pipeline? *Journal of Personality and Social Psychology, 69*, 1013–1027.

Friese, M., Hofmann, W., & Schmitt, M. (2008). When and why do implicit measures predict behavior? Empirical evidence for the moderating role of opportunity, motivation, and process reliance. *European Review of Social Psychology, 19*, 285–338.

Funder, D. C. (2001). Personality. *Annual Review of Psychology, 52*, 197–221.

Greenwald, A. G., & Farnham, S. D. (2000). Using the Implicit Association Test to measure self-esteem and self-concept. *Journal of Personality and Social Psychology, 79*, 1022–1038.

Kline, R. B. (2005). *Principles and practice of structural equation modeling*. New York: Guilford.

Lakes, K. D., & Hoyt, W. T. (2008). What sources contribute to variance in observer ratings? Using generalizability theory to assess construct validity of psychological measures. *Infant & Child Development, 17*, 269–284.

Leary, M. R., & MacDonald, G. (2003). Individual differences in self-esteem: A review and theoretical integration. In M. R. Leary & T. J. Tangney (Eds.), *Handbook of self and identity* (pp. 3–14). New York: Guilford.

Mischel, W. (1968). *Personality and assessment*. New York: Wiley.

Pennebaker, J. W., Francis, M. E., & Booth, R. J. (2001). *Linguistic inquiry and word count (LIWC): LIWC 2001*. Mahwah, NJ: Erlbaum.

Riketta, M., & Gebauer, J. (2009). Loving oneself deep inside: Implicit self-esteem is higher than explicit self-esteem. Manuscript submitted for publication.

 © 2010 Hogrefe Publishing

Rudolph, A., Schröder-Abé, M., Schütz, A., Gregg, A. P., & Sedikides, C. (2008). Through a glass, less darkly? Reassessing convergent and discriminant validity in measures of implicit self-esteem. *European Journal of Psychological Assessment, 24*, 273–281.

Schröder-Abé, M., Rudolph, A., & Schütz, A. (2007). High implicit self-esteem is not necessarily advantageous: Discrepancies between explicit and implicit self-esteem and their relationship with anger expression and psychological health. *European Journal of Personality, 21*, 319–339.

Schröder-Abé, M., Rudolph, A., Wiesner, A., & Schütz, A. (2007). Self-esteem discrepancies and defensive reactions to social feedback. *International Journal of Psychology, 42*, 174–183.

Schütz, A., & Sellin, I. (2006). Die Multidimensionale Selbstwertskala (MSWS) [The multidimensional self-esteem scale]. Göttingen: Hogrefe.

Spalding, L. R., & Hardin, C. D. (1999). Unconscious unease and self-handicapping: Behavioral consequences of individual differences in implicit and explicit self-esteem. *Psychological Science, 10*, 535–539.

Steffens, M. C., & Schulze König, S. (2006). Predicting spontaneous Big Five behavior with Implicit Association Tests. *European Journal of Psychological Assessment, 22*, 13–20.

Strack, F., & Deutsch, R. (2004). Reflective and impulsive determinants of social behavior. *Personality and Social Psychology Review, 8*, 220–247.

Vazire, S., & Mehl, M. R. (2008). Knowing me, knowing you: The accuracy and unique predictive validity of self-ratings and other-ratings of daily behavior. *Journal of Personality and Social Psychology, 95*, 1202–1216.

Wolf, M., Horn, A. B., Mehl, M. R. H., Haug, S., Pennebaker, J. W., & Kordy, H. (2008). Computergestützte quantitative Textanalyse. Äquivalenz und Robustheit der deutschen Version des Linguistic Inquiry and Word Count [Computer-aided quantitative text analysis: Equivalence and reliability of the German adaptation of the linguistic inquiry and word count]. *Diagnostica, 54*, 85–98.

Almut Rudolph

Department of Psychology
Chemnitz University of Technology
Wilhelm-Raabe-Str. 43
D-09107 Chemnitz
Germany
Tel. +49 371 531 35781
Fax +49 371 531 27459
E-mail almut.rudolph@psychologie.tu-chemnitz.de

© 2010 Hogrefe Publishing 

Original Article

# Convergence of Direct, Indirect, and Objective Risk-Taking Measures in Gambling

## The Moderating Role of Impulsiveness and Self-Control

Friederike X. R. Dislich,[1] Axel Zinkernagel,[1] Tuulia M. Ortner,[2] and Manfred Schmitt[1]

[1]University of Koblenz-Landau, Germany
[2]Free University Berlin, Germany

**Abstract.** Based on dual-process models, we assumed that risk taking depends on implicit and explicit risk attitudes and risk propensity. Specifically, we predicted that the convergence between these indicators would depend on the impulsiveness versus reflectiveness of risk behavior. Two objective personality tests (OPTs) of risk taking that measure risk behavior in standardized situations were employed. We predicted that the impulsive OPT would depend more on implicit risk dispositions. The reverse effect pattern was expected for the reflective OPT. Next, we expected that self-control would amplify the weight of explicit dispositions and attenuate that of implicit dispositions. At Time 1, two direct questionnaire measures of explicit risk proneness, three indirect measures of implicit risk proneness, and a self-control measure were administered. At Time 2, participants participated in a reflective and an impulsive gambling OPT. The assumed pattern of effects was obtained. We conclude with a discussion of future research avenues.

**Keywords:** objective personality tests, Implicit Association Test, Semantic Misattribution Procedure, predictive validity of indirect measures

Researchers have long been interested in understanding the psychological aspects of risky behavior (Kogan & Wallach, 1964). Two main lines of thinking have been pursued. Some scholars have assumed that risk propensity is a specific personality trait with strong biological roots (Zuckerman, 1991). Other researchers have used action theories such as the Ajzen and Fishbein (1977) theory of reasoned action for explaining risk taking. According to this theory, risk taking results from decisions that are strongly influenced by attitudes toward risk taking. Furthermore, it is assumed that attitudes toward risk taking result from expectations about the consequences of risk taking and the value of these consequences. Both theoretical models have stimulated the development of instruments for measuring risk attitudes and risk propensity. For many years, self-report questionnaires were used almost exclusively for this purpose. The reliance on self-report measures has been criticized for the well-known weaknesses of these measures (Hunt, Hopko, Bare, Lejuez, & Robinson, 2005). The two most critical weaknesses of self-report measures are their fakeability and people's limited self-knowledge. In response to these issues, alternative measurement techniques have been proposed. Among these are indirect measures and objective personality tests (OPTs).

Over the last two decades, the development of indirect measures has made great progress (Fazio & Olson, 2003). The currently most widely used indirect procedures employ response time measures for priming effects (Fazio, Sanbonmatsu, Powell, & Kardes, 1986) and implicit associations (e.g., De Houwer, 2006). Reaction time procedures have been used as indirect measures of risk propensity in various domains such as alcohol (ab)use (e.g., Thush et al., 2009), unsafe sex (e.g., Czopp, Monteith, Zimmerman, & Lynam, 2004), unhealthy food choices (e.g., Friese, Hofmann, & Wänke, 2008), and implicit risk attitudes (e.g., Ronay & Kim, 2006).

OPTs were first proposed by Cattell and Warburton (1967). OPTs directly measure the behavior of an individual in standardized situations. Ideally, these techniques employ unobvious tasks or scoring algorithms that prevent faking. During the last decade, several OPTs for measuring risk propensity have been proposed. Among these are the two OPTs that we used in this study: the Balloon Analog Risk Task (BART; Lejuez et al., 2002) and the Game of Dice Task (GDT; Brand et al., 2005).

Little is known about how these OPTs converge with direct and indirect measures of explicit and implicit risk attitudes and risk propensity. The present research was


DOI: 10.1027/0044-3409/a000004
© 2010 Hogrefe Publishing

conducted to fill this gap. More specifically, we tested specific hypotheses on the *moderated* convergence of these measures. Our hypotheses were derived from a theoretical model that has been developed to account for the variable implicit-explicit consistency and the variable predictive validity of direct and indirect measures (Friese, Hofmann, & Schmitt, 2008; Hofmann, Gschwendner, Nosek, & Schmitt, 2005). In the present study we tested whether this model was able to account for the variable convergence among direct, indirect, and objective risk measures.

In line with other dual-process theories (for an overview see Smith & Decoster, 2000), our model assumes that implicit and explicit dispositions are structurally distinct albeit interrelated constructs. Implicit dispositions are conceived of as associative networks of concepts. For instance, a positive implicit risk attitude is thought to be represented in memory as an association between the concept of "risk" and positive concepts such as "exciting." Accordingly, an implicit self-concept of high risk propensity is assumed to be represented in memory as an association between the concept of "self" and the concept of "risk taker." Associative networks that represent implicit dispositions can be activated automatically, quickly, and without the use of cognitive resources. Because people have no conscious awareness of the relevant associations, implicit dispositions can only be measured indirectly by tasks that are either facilitated or inhibited by the activation of concepts. By contrast, explicit dispositions are assumed to be represented in a propositional format and accessible to introspection. They are part of a person's conscious self-knowledge and they can therefore be measured directly via self-report questionnaires.

Importantly in the present context, our model and other dual-process models assume that controlled behavior depends more strongly on explicit traits, whereas automatic behavior is influenced more strongly by implicit dispositions. In fact, research in the domain of shyness has demonstrated a complete double dissociation with indirect measures of implicit shyness, predicting only automatic behavior but not controlled behavior, and direct measures of explicit shyness, predicting only controlled behavior but not automatic behavior (Asendorpf, Banse, & Mücke, 2002).

We applied this assumption of dual-process theories to risk taking and tested it by using two different OPTs, one that can be seen as a task gratifying impulsive and punishing reflective tendencies (impulsive OPT), and one that gratifies reflective and punishes impulsive behavior (reflective OPT). The impulsive OPT thus serves as an indicator of more automatic risk behavior, and the reflective OPT serves as an indicator of more controlled risk behavior.

Besides the automaticity versus controllability of behavior, our model includes a number of additional moderators that are assumed to affect the amount of convergence among implicit and explicit traits, and, accordingly, the amount of convergence among their indirect, direct, and behavioral indicators. One of these moderators, self-control, is of special interest here. This is true because self-control dilemmas often result from conflicts between automatic (impulsive) and controlled (reflective) action tendencies (Carver, 2005). Self-control has been defined as the capacity to override or inhibit "undesired behavioral tendencies (such as impulses) and to refrain from acting on them" (Tangney, Baumeister, & Boone, 2004, p. 4). Accordingly, when self-control is high, behavioral decisions rely more strongly on explicit dispositions. By contrast, if self-control is low, behavior will be affected more strongly by implicit dispositions.

Applying this reasoning to risk taking, we predicted that risky behavior would depend more strongly on explicit risk dispositions for people high in self-control as compared to people low in self-control. Accordingly, we predicted that risk-taking behavior would depend more strongly on implicit risk dispositions for people low in self-control as compared to people high in self-control.

## Hypotheses and Overview of Research

Combining our reasoning on the moderator effects of automaticity (vs. controllability) of behavior and self-control resulted in six hypotheses:

(1) Compared to direct measures of explicit risk dispositions, indirect measures of implicit risk dispositions will be better predictors of an impulsive OPT.
(2) Compared to indirect measures of implicit risk dispositions, direct measures of explicit risk dispositions will be better predictors of a reflective OPT.
(3) Indirect measures of implicit risk dispositions (attitude and risk propensity) will predict an impulsive OPT better than a reflective OPT.
(4) Direct measures of explicit risk dispositions will predict a reflective OPT better than an impulsive OPT.
(5) Self-control will attenuate the capacity of indirect measures of implicit risk dispositions to predict behavior in risk OPTs.
(6) Self-control will amplify the capacity of direct measures of explicit risk dispositions to predict behavior in risk OPTs.

The major goal of our study was to test these hypotheses. Because little is known so far about the psychometric quality of indirect measures of implicit risk dispositions, a second goal of our study was to compare several indirect measures. The first indirect measure was a semantic version (cf. Banse, Imhoff, Schmidt, & Bernhardt, submitted) of the Affective Misattribution Procedure (AMP; Payne, Cheng, Govorun, & Stewart, 2005). We call this procedure the Semantic Misattribution Procedure (SMP). The second indirect measure was a classical Implicit Association Test (IAT; Greenwald, McGhee, & Schwartz, 1998). The third indirect measure was a Single-Category IAT (SC-IAT; Karpinski & Steinmann, 2006). The SMP and the SC-IAT were designed to measure the implicit association between gambling and risk. The IAT was designed to measure a participant's implicit self-concept of being a risk-prone person.

As a first direct measure of explicit risk disposition, we employed a German version (Johnson, Wilke, & Weber, 2004) of the Domain-Specific Risk-Taking Scale

© 2010 Hogrefe Publishing

(DOSPERT; Blais & Weber, 2001). As a second direct measure of explicit risk disposition, we employed ratings of the risk stimuli that were used in the IAT and the SMP. Participants were asked to rate how risky they found various types of gambling. Finally, for OPTs we used the GDT (Brand et al., 2005) and the BART (Lejuez et al., 2002). The GDT was used as a measure of more reflective risk taking. It was developed to measure decisions under risk when the probabilities of winning or losing are obvious (Brand et al., 2005). Accordingly, thoughtful decisions are associated with advantageous decision making in that task (Brand, Heinze, Labudda, & Markowitsch, 2008). The BART was developed as a measure of more impulsive risk taking. Accordingly, Lejuez et al. (2002) found significant correlations between the BART and impulsivity.

# Method

## Participants

One hundred twelve students (90 women and 22 men) between 18 and 29 years of age ($M$ = 22.04, $SD$ = 3.6) participated in exchange for research participation credit or monetary compensation.

## Measures

### SMP

Risky words from the domain of gambling (roulette) and safe words (shelter) were presented as primes for 75 ms, followed by a blank screen for 125 ms and a Chinese pictograph (target) for 100 ms. Following the Chinese pictograph, a pattern mask consisting of black and white noise appeared until the participant responded. The next trial began as soon as participants made a response. Participants were asked to rate the pictographs either as "risky" or as "safe." Following the instructions proposed by Payne et al. (2005), participants were asked to ignore the primes that allegedly just served as signals. In addition, they were warned that the primes could actually bias their evaluation of the Chinese character and that they should try their hardest not to be influenced. The SMP consisted of two blocks, in which 20 different primes were used for each category in a random order. Each prime was presented twice, once in both blocks. A person's SMP score equals the percentage of risky choices after gambling primes. High (low) SMP scores indicate strong (weak) associations between gambling and risk and thus represent implicit safety (risk) proneness. Reliability was estimated as the Spearman-Brown-corrected correlation between SMP test halves ($\alpha$ = .71).

### IAT

The IAT was explained to participants as a categorization task in which they were to react as quickly as possible to the stimuli presented according to the category label assignments at the top of the screen. Each combined block consisted of 60 trails. In the first combined block, participants had to respond with the same key to "me" words as to "secure" words. The "secure" words were the same as employed in the SMP. The second key was used for the classification of "other" words and "risky" words. The "risky" words were the same as were used in the SMP. In the second combined block, the key assignment for "risky" and "secure" words was reversed. The order of block assignment was kept constant for each participant (cf. Egloff & Schmukle, 2002). Following Greenwald, Nosek, and Banaji (2003), data from the combined blocks were used to compute IAT scores. Positive values indicate faster reactions when "me" and "secure" words shared the same response key as compared to when "me" and "risky" words shared the same response key. High (low) IAT scores indicate strong (weak) associations between self and risk and thus represent an implicit safety (risk) self-concept. Internal consistency was computed using four parcels of mutually exclusive IAT trials ($\alpha$ = .88).

### SC-IAT

All procedural details of the SC-IAT were identical to the IAT except that only a single target category rather than two target categories (SC-IAT; Karpinski & Steinman, 2006) and different attribute categories were used. This single target category was "gambling." The words that represented this category were the same words that we used as risky primes in the SMP. As attribute stimuli, we used three words representing the attribute category "loss" and three words representing the attribute category "gain." Combined blocks consisted of 75 trials. High (low) SC-IAT scores indicate strong (weak) associations between gambling and risk and thus represent implicit safety (risk) proneness. Internal consistency across four subsets of SC-IAT scores amounted to $\alpha$ = .79.

### DOSPERT-G

The DOSPERT-G (Johnson et al., 2004) consists of three scales with four items each: (a) The risk-perception scale measures a participant's risk perception of four kinds of gambling (sports betting, poker, betting in horse races, and casino gambling); (b) The expected-benefit scale measures a person's expected benefit from these types of gambling; and (c) The third scale measures a person's likelihood of engaging in each of these gambling activities. Responses were given on 5-point rating scales. Responses were coded such that high (low) scores indicate strong (weak) explicit associations between gambling and risk, weak (strong) explicit associations between gambling and benefit, and a low (high) risk propensity. All correlations between the scales exceeded .80. Therefore, the scales were combined ($\alpha$ = .84).

### Explicit Risk Rating

The risky words that were used as primes in the SMP and as target stimuli in the IAT and the SC-IAT were explicitly

 © 2010 Hogrefe Publishing

rated as secure versus risky using bipolar 6-point rating scales (α = .88). High (low) scores indicate strong (weak) explicit associations between gambling and risk and thus a low (high) risk propensity.

### Self-Control Scale

The self-control scale of a questionnaire for measuring self-control resources was used (FSSTK; Schmidt, in preparation). The scale consists of 10 items that are rated on 5-point scales ranging from 1 to 5 (α = .86). Item example: I have difficulty controlling my impulses. Responses were coded such that high scores indicate strong self-control.

### BART

At the start of the BART (Lejuez et al., 2002), the computer screen displayed three items: a small balloon accompanied by a balloon pump labeled *Click here to pump up the balloon*, a reset button labeled *Collect $$$*, and a *Total Score*. Each click on the pump inflated the balloon 1° (about 0.32 cm) in all directions. With each pump, money (€0.01 per pump) was accumulated in a temporary bank, the holdings of which were not indicated to the participant. When a balloon was pumped past its individual explosion point, the computer generated a popping sound. When a balloon exploded, all money in the temporary bank was lost, and a new balloon appeared on the screen. At any point during each balloon trial, a participant could stop pumping the balloon by clicking the *Collect $$$* button. Clicking this button transferred all money from the temporary bank to the permanent bank, at which time the new total earned would be incrementally updated while a slot machine payoff sound played to confirm payment. A new balloon appeared after each balloon explosion or money collection until a total of 10 balloons (i.e., trials) were completed. The probability that a balloon would explode was fixed at 1/128 for the first pump. If the balloon did not explode after the first pump, the probability that the balloon would explode was 1/127 on the second pump, and so on, until the 128th pump at which point the probability of an explosion was 1/1 (i.e., 100%). According to this algorithm, the average explosion point was 64 pumps. Modeling real-world situations in which excessive risk often produces diminishing returns and increasing threats, each successive pump on any particular balloon trial increased the amount to be lost from a pump. Detailed instructions provided to the participant were based on those provided by Lejuez et al. (2002, pp. 78–79), yet it is important to note that participants were given no precise information about the probability of an explosion. Although there are several potential dependent measures, we analyzed the total money earned (BART score). Other variables such as number of explosions, maximum number of pumps of a balloon, and (un-)adjusted average number of pumps produced similar findings. Higher BART scores indicate higher levels of impulsive risk taking. Reliability was estimated as the Spearman-Brown-corrected correlation between BART test halves (α = .69).

### GDT

The GDT (Brand et al., 2005) is a computerized decision-making task that provides – in contrast to the BART – explicit information about the gains and losses associated with a given choice. Participants are instructed to maximize their fictitious starting capital of €1,000 within 10 throws of a single virtual die. Before each throw, they have to guess which number will be thrown next. Different options for the decision are offered, each of which has a different winning probability (ranging from 16.6% to 66.6%) and is related to a specific amount of gain or loss (ranging from €1,000 for the most improbable choice to €100 for the option most likely to lead to a win). For instance, before the die is rolled, participants have the option of choosing one single number with a winning probability of 1:6 (16.6%), which will result in high gain of €1,000 when the chosen number is thrown, but also a loss of €1,000 when one of the other five numbers is thrown. They also have the choice of choosing a combination of two numbers, which produces a gain of €500 when one of these two numbers is thrown (winning probability 1:3 = 33.3%), but also a loss of €500 when one of the remaining numbers occurs. Another option is to choose a combination of three numbers, which is associated with a gain of €200 (when one of these numbers is thrown) or a loss of €200 (overall winning probability of 50%). Lastly, participants can choose a combination of four numbers (e.g., 2, 3, 4, and 5 together with a winning probability of 66.6%), which will lead to a gain of only €100 in the case that one of the four numbers is thrown, but also a loss of €100 in the case that one of the other two numbers is thrown. Before the task, participants are explicitly briefed about the rules for gains and losses, as well as the amounts of money associated with each of the different possible options that they may choose. Moreover, the rules are permanently presented on the screen. Subjects have to make a total of 10 decisions within the game. After each throw, the gain or loss is indicated on the screen. The computer also displays the participant's current money total, as well as the number of remaining rounds. In the GDT, two out of the four possible choices (the three number combination and the four number combination) are defined as "advantageous" since they have a winning probability of 50% or higher and are associated with low losses. The other two options are referred to as "disadvantageous" since they have a winning probability of less than 50% and result in high losses. The GDT score is defined by the amount of money accrued after the tenth round. Higher GDT scores indicate lower reflective risk taking. Reliability was estimated by the Spearman-Brown-corrected correlation between GDT test halves (α = .68).

## Procedure

The study consisted of two sessions with a time lapse of 2 weeks. The study was conducted in the laboratory in groups of up to five individuals. Upon arrival, participants were greeted by an experimenter and seated at individual computer stations. In the first session, participants completed

© 2010 Hogrefe Publishing

the three indirect risk propensity measures, the two direct risk propensity measures, and the self-control scale. Two weeks later, participants completed the two OPTs. A code number for each participant assured anonymity while enabling the combination of data from both occasions of measurement. After all data had been collected, participants were fully debriefed and thanked for their participation.

# Results

## Descriptive Statistics and Correlations Between the Measures

Table 1 reports the descriptive statistics for all measures. Correlations between the measures are given in Table 2. Note that all risk measures, except the BART, are coded such that high scores correspond to low risk. Accordingly, high self-control scores indicate strong self-control. By contrast, high BART scores indicate high risk. The signs for all correlations were as expected. More specifically, the BART had negative correlations with all other risk measures and a negative correlation with self-control. All risk measures besides the BART correlated positively with each other and with self-control.

The correlations among the three indirect risk measures were not significant ($p > .05$) and ranged from $r = .06$ to $r = .15$. The correlation between the two direct risk measures was significant ($p < .05$) and amounted to $r = .19$. The correlation between the two OPTs was not significant although the sign of the correlation was as expected ($r = -.20$). Of the six correlations between the three indirect risk measures and the two direct risk measures, one was significant: The SMP had a positive correlation with the DOSPERT-G scale ($r = .21$, $p < .05$). Of the six correlations between the three indirect risk measures and the two OPTs, one was significant: the SC-IAT had a negative correlation with the BART ($r = -.33$, $p < .01$). Of the four correlations between the two direct risk measures and the two OPTs, two were significant: the GDT had a positive correlation both with the DOSPERT-G scale ($r = .33$, $p < .01$) and with the explicit rating ($r = .23$, $p < .05$).

## Multiple Regression Analyses

In order to test our first four hypotheses, the two OPTs were regressed in separate analyses on all direct and indirect risk measures. In the first analysis with the impulsive OPT (BART) as the dependent variable, a significant effect of the SC-IAT, $\beta = -.33$, $t(110) = 3.59$, $p < .01$, was obtained. No other predictor had a significant effect. Thus, Hypothesis 1 received support in that only an indirect measure of implicit risk proneness had a significant effect.

In the second analysis with the reflective OPT (GDT) as the dependent variable, a significant main effect of the DOSPERT-G scale was obtained, $\beta = .33$, $t(110) = 3.50$, $p < .01$. No other predictor had a significant effect. Thus, Hypothesis 2 received support in that only a direct measure of explicit risk disposition had a significant effect.

Results for the two regression analyses were also consistent with Hypotheses 3 and 4. Indirect measures of implicit risk dispositions predicted the impulsive OPT better than the reflective OPT (Hypothesis 3). Direct measures of explicit risk dispositions predicted the reflective OPT better than the impulsive OPT (Hypothesis 4).

## Moderated Regression Analyses

Hypotheses 5 and 6 were tested via moderated regression analysis using product terms from the centered predictor and moderator variables (Aiken & West, 1991). Moderator analyses were performed only for those risk measures that had turned out to be predictive in the previous analyses. More specifically, we tested whether self-control moderated (reduced) the effect of the SC-IAT on the OPTs

*Table 1*. Descriptive statistics of the measures

| | # | α | *M* | *SD* | Min | Max |
|---|---|---|---|---|---|---|
| *Indirect measures* | | | | | | |
| 1. SMP | n.a. | .71 | 52.63 | 11.37 | 13 | 80 |
| 2. Classical IAT | n.a. | .88 | 0.45 | 0.27 | −0.34 | 1.65 |
| 3. SC-IAT | n.a. | .79 | 0.44 | 0.34 | −0.43 | 1.78 |
| *Direct measures* | | | | | | |
| 4. DOSPERT-G | 12 | .84 | 28.23 | 8.64 | 12 | 60 |
| 5. Explicit rating | 5 | .88 | 13.17 | 3.31 | 6 | 30 |
| *Moderator* | | | | | | |
| 6. Self-control scale | 10 | .86 | 31.71 | 7.59 | 13 | 49 |
| *OPTs* | | | | | | |
| 7. BART | 10 | .69 | 196.35 | 53.26 | 65 | 381 |
| 8. GDT | 10 | .68 | 1161.61 | 584.98 | −300 | 2,800 |

*Note*. # = number of items; α = internal consistency.

 © 2010 Hogrefe Publishing

*Table 2.* Correlations between the measures

| | 1 | 2 | 3 | 4 | 5 | 6 | 7 |
|---|---|---|---|---|---|---|---|
| *Indirect measures* | | | | | | | |
| 1. SMP | | | | | | | |
| 2. Classical IAT | .15 | | | | | | |
| 3. SC-IAT | .06 | .09 | | | | | |
| *Direct measures* | | | | | | | |
| 4. DOSPERT-G | .21* | .09 | .04 | | | | |
| 5. Explicit rating | .11 | .01 | .02 | .19* | | | |
| *Moderator* | | | | | | | |
| 6. Self-control scale | .15 | .06 | .18 | .14 | .30** | | |
| *OPTs* | | | | | | | |
| 7. BART | −.01 | −.16 | −.33** | −.17 | −.07 | −.31** | |
| 8. GDT | .09 | .02 | .03 | .33** | .23* | .33** | −.20 |

*$p < .05$; **$p < .01$.

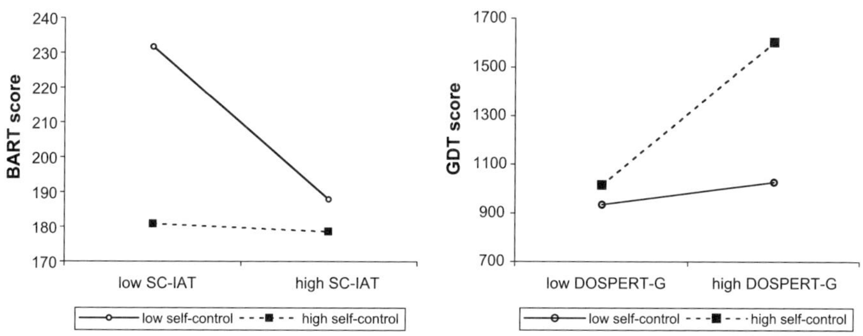


*Figure 1.* Moderator effect of self-control on the BART (left panel) and on the GDT (right panel).

(Hypothesis 5) and whether self-control moderated (amplified) the effect of the DOSPERT-G scale on the OPTs (Hypothesis 6).

When testing Hypothesis 5, a significant main effect of the SC-IAT, $\beta = -.28$, $t(108)$, $p < .01$, a significant main effect of self-control, $\beta = -.22$, $t(108)$, $p < .05$, and a significant moderator effect of self-control were found for the SC-IAT as a predictor of the BART, $\beta = .19$, $t(108)$, $p < .05$. As can be seen from the conditional expectations in Figure 1 (left panel), the effect of the SC-IAT on the BART was stronger for people low in self-control than for people high in self-control.

When testing Hypothesis 6, a significant main effect of the DOSPERT-G, $\beta = .29$, $t(108)$, $p < .01$, a significant main effect of self-control, $\beta = .28$, $t(108)$, $p < .01$, and a significant moderator effect of self-control were found for the DOSPERT-G scale as a predictor of the GDT, $\beta = .21$, $t(108)$, $p < .01$. As can be seen from the conditional expectations in Figure 1 (right panel), the effect of the DOSPERT-G scale on the GDT was stronger for people high in self-control than for people low in self-control.

## Discussion

To our knowledge, the present paper reports the first attempt to explore the moderated convergence of three types of risk proneness indicators: direct self-report measures of explicit risk disposition, indirect measures of implicit risk disposition, and OPTs that measure risk behavior in well-defined tasks.

The results of our study are fully consistent with our theoretical reasoning. The BART, an impulsive risk OPT, was predicted by an SC-IAT that measures implicit attitudes toward gambling indirectly. Direct measures of risk attitudes and risk propensity had no effect on this OPT. By contrast, the GDT, a reflective risk OPT, was predicted by the DOSPERT-G scale that measures explicit attitudes toward gambling directly. Indirect measures of risk attitudes and risk propensity were not predictive of the reflective OPT. Finally, and as predicted, self-control attenuated the effect of the indirect measure of risk attitudes and amplified the effect of the direct measure of risk attitudes. Although the results of our study support our theoretical assumptions, they leave open important questions that need to be addressed in additional research.

A first issue is the low convergence among the indirect measures of implicit risk propensity. Even though the reliability of the three measures that we designed was satisfactory, none of the correlations among the indirect measures was significant. Low convergence among indirect measures is a common observation, especially in the domain of self-esteem (Rudolph, Schröder-Abé, Schütz, Gregg, & Sedikides, 2008), and the reasons for this result are not yet well understood. The procedures we used were designed

© 2010 Hogrefe Publishing 

to measure distinct but related constructs. The SMP and the SC-IAT were intended to measure implicit associations between gambling and risk, the IAT was designed to measure implicit associations between self and risk. The pattern of correlations does not reflect this communality between the SMP and the SC-IAT, or their distinctiveness from the IAT. Partly, this may result from differences in the underlying mechanism of the SMP and the SC-IAT. Whereas the SC-IAT employs response interference as the core mechanism, the SMP does not. Thus, while the low convergence between the IAT and the other two indirect measures may reflect the distinctiveness of the measured constructs, the low convergence between the SMP and the SC-IAT may reflect procedural differences between both measures and differences in the mechanisms they capture. In future studies, underlying mechanisms, procedural aspects, and constructs to be measured have to be varied more systematically and, ideally, in a fully crossed design. Such a strategy would help in identifying sources of systematic and unsystematic variance, and sources of covariance. Structural equation models should be employed to partition the variances of the measures into substantive and procedural sources (Blanton, Jaccard, Gonzales, & Christie, 2006).

Second, small correlations were observed between indirect and direct risk measures. Again, this pattern is not unusual and it has been interpreted by some authors as evidence of discriminant validity. This interpretation is unsafe, however, because the low correlation between direct and indirect measures of explicit and implicit constructs may result from two factors that cannot be separated. The low correlations may reflect distinctiveness on the level of constructs. In this case, the low correlation would indeed indicate discriminant validity of the measures. However, the correlations may also reflect low convergent construct validity. In this case, the low correlation on the level of the measures would not match with the overlap of the constructs. Unfortunately, the two interpretations cannot be disentangled. Constructs (explicit and implicit) cannot be fully crossed with measures (direct and indirect) because implicit constructs cannot be measured directly, and because explicit self-knowledge cannot be measured indirectly with procedures such as the IAT or the SMP (Gschwendner, Hofmann, & Schmitt, 2008). We are not aware of a convincing solution to this fundamental problem.

Third, the two OPTs did not correlate significantly with each other. Again, the reasons for this result are not clear. Because lack of reliability can be ruled out as an explanation, it seems justified for the time being to assume that both OPTs indeed measure different types of risk taking, namely impulsive risk taking and reflective risk taking. This interpretation matches our hypotheses and the empirical results we obtained. It seems difficult to come up with an alternative interpretation that would explain the entire pattern of results as well as our theoretical model does. In this regard, our research seems promising. It seems worthwhile to continue employing OPTs in addition to self-report questionnaires and indirect measures such as the ones we have used.

Fourth, we included only two moderators in our design: impulsiveness and self-control. Our model contains many more moderators, such as trait importance, self-knowledge, social desirability concerns, and cognitive control resources, to mention some. In other studies, we have shown that these moderators have an impact on both the degree of implicit-explicit consistency and the predictive validity of direct and indirect measures vis à vis behavioral outcomes (Friese et al., 2008; Hofmann et al., 2005). Including additional moderators seems to be an important task for future studies.

Fifth, we measured self-control only explicitly. Not surprisingly, the self-control questionnaire that we used had correlations with the two explicit risk measures. In order to obtain a symmetric pattern of measures (direct and indirect) and constructs (explicit and implicit), not only on the level of the substantive construct at issue (risk taking), but on the level of moderators as well, future studies should more systematically include indirect measures of implicit moderator constructs. As far as we can tell from our knowledge of the literature, the fully symmetric design we suggest has never been performed.

Sixth, one of our moderators, impulsiveness, varied between behaviors, whereas the other moderator, self-control, varied between individuals. As we have argued earlier (Friese et al., 2008), testing moderator hypotheses should ideally employ three types of functionally equivalent factors: personality factors, situation factors, and types of behavior. Including these three types of functionally equivalent moderators has two advantages: First, moderator constructs can be replicated across sources of variance; second, it allows for testing whether personality factors, situation factors, and types of behavior have additive or interactive moderator effects (Schmitt, 2009).

## Acknowledgments

We thank Jane Thompson and two anonymous reviewers for helpful comments on this paper, and Martha Haider, Matthias Hunn, and Benjamin Stahl for their help in data collection.

# References

Aiken, L. S., & West, S. G. (1991). *Multiple regression: Testing and interpreting interactions*. Newbury Park, NJ: Sage.

Ajzen, I., & Fishbein, M. (1977). Attitude-behavior relations: A theoretical analysis and review of empirical research. *Psychological Bulletin, 84*, 888–918.

Asendorpf, J. B., Banse, R., & Mücke, D. (2002). Double dissociation between implicit and explicit personality self-concept: The case of shy behavior. *Journal of Personality and Social Psychology, 83*, 380–393.

Banse, R., Imhoff, R., Schmidt, A. F., & Bernhardt, J. (submitted). An inkblot for male sexual preference: The sexual misattribution procedure.

Blais, A.-R., & Weber, E. U. (2001). A domain-specific risk-taking (DOSPERT) scale for adult populations. *Judgement and Decision Making, 1*, 33–47.

Blanton, H., Jaccard, J., Gonzales, P. M., & Christie, C. (2006). Decoding the implicit association test: Implications for criterion prediction. *Journal of Experimental Social Psychology, 42*, 192–212.

 © 2010 Hogrefe Publishing

Brand, M., Fujiwara, E., Borsutzky, S., Kalbe, E., Kessler, J., & Markowitsch, H. J. (2005). Decision-making deficits of Korsakoff patients in a new gambling task with explicit rules: Associations with executive functions. *Neuropsychology, 19*, 267–277.

Brand, M., Heinze, K., Labudda, K., & Markowitsch, H. J. (2008). The role of strategies in deciding advantageously in ambiguous and risky situations. *Cognitive Processing, 9*, 159–173.

Carver, C. S. (2005). Impulse and constraint: Perspectives from personality psychology, convergence with theory in other areas, and potential for integration. *Personality and Social Psychology Review, 9*, 312–333.

Cattell, R. B., & Warburton, F. W. (1967). *Objective personality and motivation tests: A theoretical introduction and practical compendium*. Champaign, IL: University of Illinois Press.

Czopp, A. M., Monteith, M. J., Zimmerman, R. S., & Lynam, D. R. (2004). Implicit attitudes as potential protection from risky sex: Predicting condom use with the IAT. *Basic and Applied Social Psychology, 26*, 227–236.

De Houwer, J. (2006). Using the Implicit Association Test does not rule out an impact of conscious propositional knowledge on evaluative conditioning. *Learning and Motivation, 37*, 176–187.

Egloff, B., & Schmukle, S. C. (2002). Predictive validity of an Implicit Association Test for assessing anxiety. *Journal of Personality and Social Psychology, 83*, 1441–1455.

Fazio, R. H., & Olson, M. A. (2003). Implicit measures in social cognition research: Their meaning and uses. *Annual Review of Psychology, 54*, 297–327.

Fazio, R. H., Sanbonmatsu, D. M., Powell, M. C., & Kardes, F. R. (1986). On the automatic activation of attitudes. *Journal of Personality and Social Psychology, 50*, 229–238.

Friese, M., Hofmann, W., & Schmitt, M. (2008). When and why do implicit measures predict behavior? Empirical evidence for the moderating role of opportunity, motivation, and process reliance. *European Review of Social Psychology, 19*, 285–338.

Friese, M., Hofmann, W., & Wänke, M. (2008). When impulses take over: Moderated predictive validity of implicit and explicit attitude measures in predicting food choice and consumption behavior. *British Journal of Social Psychology, 47*, 397–419.

Greenwald, A. G., McGhee, D. E., & Schwartz, J. L. (1998). Measuring individual differences in implicit cognition: The Implicit Association Test. *Journal of Personality and Social Psychology, 74*, 1464–1480.

Greenwald, A. G., Nosek, B. A., & Banaji, M. R. (2003). Understanding and using the Implicit Association Test I: An improved scoring algorithm. *Journal of Personality and Social Psychology, 85*, 197–216.

Gschwendner, T., Hofmann, W., & Schmitt, M. (2008). Convergent and predictive validity of implicit and explicit anxiety measures as a function of specificity similarity and content similarity. *European Journal of Psychological Assessment, 24*, 254–262.

Hofmann, W., Gschwendner, T., Nosek, B., & Schmitt, M. (2005). What moderates implicit-explicit consistency? *European Review of Social Psychology, 16*, 335–390.

Hunt, M. K., Hopko, D. R., Bare, R., Lejeuz, C. W., & Robinson, E. V. (2005). Construct validity of the Balloon Analog Risk Task (BART): Associations with psychopathy and impulsivity. *Assessment, 12*, 416–428.

Johnson, J. G., Wilke, A., & Weber, E. U. (2004). A domain-specific scale measuring risk perceptions, expected benefits, and perceived-risk attitude in German-speaking populations. *Polish Psychological Bulletin, 35*, 153–163.

Karpinski, A., & Steinman, R. B. (2006). The single category implicit association test as a measure of implicit social cognition. *Journal of Personality and Social Psychology, 91*, 16–32.

Kogan, N., & Wallach, M. A. (1964). *Risk taking: A study in cognition and personality*. New York, NY: Holt, Rinehart & Winston.

Lejuez, C. W., Read, J. P., Kahler, C. W., Richards, J. B., Ramsey, S. E., & Stuart, G. L. (2002). Evaluation of a behavioral measure of risk taking: The Balloon Analogue Risk Task (BART). *Journal of Experimental Psychology, 8*, 75–84.

Payne, B. K., Cheng, C. M., Govorun, O., & Stewart, B. D. (2005). An inkblot for attitudes: Affect misattribution as implicit measurement. *Journal of Personality and Social Psychology, 89*, 277–293.

Ronay, R., & Kim, D. Y. (2006). Gender differences in explicit and implicit risk attitudes: A socially facilitated phenomenon. *British Journal of Social Psychology, 45*, 397–419.

Rudolph, A., Schröder-Abé, M., Schütz, A., Gregg, A. P., & Sedikides, C. (2008). Through a glass, less darkly? Reassessing convergent and discriminant validity in measures of implicit self-esteem. *European Journal of Psychological Assessment, 24*, 273–281.

Schmidt, A. F. (in preparation). Fragebogen zu selbststeuernden Kompetenzen (FSSTK) [Questionnaire of self-regulative competencies] University of Bonn.

Schmitt, M. (2009). Person × situation – interactions as moderators. *Journal of Research in Personality, 43*, 267.

Smith, E. C., & DeCoster, J. (2000). Dual-process models in social and cognitive psychology: Conceptual integration and links to underlying memory systems. *Personality and Social Psychology Review, 4*, 108–131.

Tangney, J. P., Baumeister, R. F., & Boone, A. L. (2004). High self-control predicts good adjustment, less pathology, better grades, and interpersonal success. *Journal of Personality, 72*, 271–324.

Thush, C., Wiers, R. W., Ames, S. L., Grenard, J. L., Sussman, S., & Stacy, A. W. (2009). Interactions between implicit and explicit cognition and working memory capacity in the prediction of alcohol use in at-risk adolescents. *Drug and Alcohol Dependence, 94*, 116–124.

Zuckerman, M. (1991). *Psychobiology of personality*. New York, NY: Cambridge University Press.

Friederike Dislich

Department of Psychology
University of Koblenz-Landau
Fortstraße 7
76829 Landau
Germany
Tel. +49 6341 280 274
Fax +49 6341 280 490
E-mail dislich@uni-landau.de

© 2010 Hogrefe Publishing 

Original Article

# The Divergence of Implicit and Explicit Consumer Evaluations

## A Multimeasure Investigation

Amy Summerville,[1] Brendon Hsieh,[2] and Nick Harrington[3]

[1]Miami University, Oxford, OH, USA
[2]University of Illinois at Urbana-Champaign, IL, USA
[3]Procter and Gamble, Cincinnati, OH, USA

**Abstract.** This research extends findings that implicit and explicit attitudes may diverge to a consumer evaluation task using multiple measures of implicit evaluation: Evaluative Movement Assessment (EMA; Brendl, Markman, & Messner, 2005) and Evaluative Priming (Fazio, Jackson, Dunton, & Williams,1995). These measures were significantly associated with each other for both positive and negative implicit attitudes. Neither measure predicted explicit liking of the product or explicit intention to purchase the product. We believe this to be the first such demonstrated divergence in a naturalistic, unconditioned consumer evaluation context. Implicit activation of the product's emotional benefit (e.g., "relaxation"), as assessed in a lexical decision task (LDT), was not associated with the EMA or evaluative priming, but was significantly associated with both explicit emotional state (e.g., relaxation) and explicit purchase intention; the latter effect was not mediated by explicit emotion.

**Keywords:** consumer attitudes, implicit measures, implicit attitudes, reaction time measures

Consumer research typically relies on explicit attitude measurement strategies such as consumer surveys or focus group methods. Explicit attitudes are most predictive of highly deliberative behaviors (Wilson, Lindsey, & Schooler, 2000), whereas most consumer decisions are made when shoppers are not fully focused on the decision process. Implicit attitudes are automatically triggered by encountering the attitude object (Bargh, Chaiken, Govender, & Pratto, 1992; Fazio, Sanbonmatsu, Powell, & Kardes,1986), meaning they will be influential even when shoppers are cognitively busy. Moreover, consumer behavior may be highly habitual: Most of us know which brand of detergent we tend to use but have likely given little thought to the reasons behind that preference. Implicit attitudes are thus highly relevant to consumer decision making (Chartrand, 2005; Dijksterhuis, Smith, vanBaaren, & Wigboldus, 2005). Indeed, subtle factors, such as a match between the first letters of one's name and of the brand name, can powerfully influence consumer preferences (Brendl, Chattopadhyay, Pelham, & Carvallo, 2005). Likewise, even incidental exposure to a brand increases preference for that brand due to nonconscious effects on brand accessibility and automatic inferences about the observed users (Ferraro, Bettman, & Chartrand, 2009). Given the importance of these nonconscious influences, consumer research needs a better understanding of implicit measurement within the consumer attitudes domain. The present research examines the interrelation of three implicit measures and investigates how they relate to commonly used explicit measures of consumer preference in an attempt to fill a current gap in research.

In addition to the intrinsic importance of consumer goods, this class of attitude objects allows for unique insights into basic implicit processes (Bargh, 2002). In particular, we examine the question of implicit and explicit attitude divergence. Implicit and explicit attitudes predict different classes of behavior (Dovidio, Kawakami, & Gaertner, 2002; McConnell & Leibold, 2001; Wilson et al., 2000) and are formed differently (DeCoster, Banner, Smith, & Semin, 2006; Rydell & McConnell, 2006; Rydell, McConnell, Mackie, & Strain, 2006). Competing theories, however, suggest a unitary attitude structure with explicit attitudes aligning with implicit attitudes except under motivational pressure, social pressure, or processing constraints (Fazio & Olson, 2003; Petty & Wegener, 1998), or because of a lack of clarity in the explicit measure (Hofmann, Gawronski, Gschwendner, Le, & Schmitt, 2005). We believe that consumer goods offer a valuable domain for an investigation of the debate about divergence. Social and motivational pressures are unlikely to influence attitudes toward mundane consumer good targets: In contrast to social and intrapersonal pressures surrounding racial attitudes, it seems unlikely that anyone experiences meaningful pressure to report positive attitudes toward particular types of dish soap. To the extent that deliberate misreporting of explicit attitudes causes a divergence between these two attitude types, we would expect greater convergence for consumer


DOI: 10.1027/0044-3409/a000005
© 2010 Hogrefe Publishing

goods, where this misreporting should be minimized (see Hofmann et al., 2005). If, however, these two systems are truly distinct, then the attitude context should not affect their divergence.

Existing research on the convergence of implicit and explicit attitude measures has focused heavily on the Implicit Association Task (Greenwald, McGhee, & Schwartz, 1998; for a recent meta-analysis, see Hofmann et al., 2005). In order not to replicate this body of work, we used two less common measures of implicit evaluation that both utilize computerized reaction time tasks: the evaluative priming paradigm (EVP; Fazio et al., 1995) and the evaluative movement assessment (EMA; Brendl, Markman, & Messner, 2005). These measures both include independent components of positive and negative attitudes or preference. Using these components independently allows a neutral response, where the individual holds *neither* strongly positive nor strongly negative feelings, to be disambiguated from an ambivalent response, in which the individual holds *both* strongly positive and strongly negative attitudes (Cacioppo & Berntson, 1994). We believe that using independent measures of these two dimensions provides greater power in determining the predictive utility of implicit measures on behavioral intentions through more sensitive measurement of attitudes likely to fall toward the midpoint of a bipolar scale.

The evaluative priming procedure (EVP; Fazio et al., 1995) examines the ability of an attitude object to prime positivity or negativity. In this procedure, the target or control object appears briefly prior to presentation of a positive or negative word. Participants are instructed to indicate if the word means "good" or "bad" using a response keypress. The degree to which the attitude object facilitates the identification of positive words as "good" represents the implicit positive evaluation, and the facilitation of identifying negative words represents the implicit negative evaluation.

The EMA (Brendl, Markman et al., 2005) is a relatively new computerized reaction time task that uses response compatibility to assess implicit attitudes. Participants use response keys to move words toward or away from their name, which appears at the center of the screen. Positive distractor words (e.g., baby and birthday) are always moved toward the name, and negative distractor words (e.g., rats and death) are always moved away from the name. A separate set of target words, representing the attitude objects, is identified before the task. These attitude objects are mixed in with the distractor words and have specific instructions per block of trials. Participants perform two blocks in which the attitude objects are moved toward the name and two blocks in which the attitude objects are moved away from the name; during these blocks, they continue to move positive words toward the name and negative words away from the name (see Figure 1 for a schematic). The mean latency to move the attitude object toward the name represents the implicit positive attitude, and the mean latency to move the attitude object away from the name represents the implicit negative attitude.

The theoretical basis of the EMA parallels work by Chen and Bargh (1999) that, like Brendl, Markman et al. (2005), has found reaction time scores from "moving" targets in relation to the self correlate with explicit evaluations of attitude objects. These movement-compatibility effects generalize across a variety of movement response types (Rotteveel & Phaf, 2004; Seibt, Neumann, Nussinson, & Strack, 2008; van Dantzig, Pecher, & Zwaan, 2008; van Dantzig, Zeelenberg, & Pecher, 2009; Wentura, Rothermund, & Bak, 2000). The Implicit Associative Procedure (IAP; Schnabel, Banse, & Asendorpf, 2006) is a joystick measure equivalent to the EMA (Markman & Brendl, 2005). An IAP assessing implicit perceptions of control over anxiety-causing events was associated with explicit measurements of anxiety (Hogendoorn et al., 2008). Likewise, Reinecke, Becker, and Rinck (in press) report in this issue that responses to phobic stimuli on the Approach-Avoidance Task (Rinck & Becker, 2007), another movement-compatibility task, relate to self-report measures of anxiety about these stimuli. Overall, these findings suggest the EMA and its kin have predictive utility for a variety of contexts.

Whereas the EMA and the EVP are both designed to measure implicit evaluations, we are also interested in assessing implicit activation of specific attributes of the target products, namely the emotional experiences the products are meant to evoke (e.g., a detergent making the user feel joyful). We therefore also included a lexical decision task (LDT; Meyer & Schvaneveldt, 1971). This task, unlike the previously discussed measures, does not involve a direct pairing of the attitude object and the target attribute within the task. Instead, it assesses general activation of the target attribute (e.g., joy) by measuring response latencies in the decision of whether a letter string represents a word (e.g., JOY and JOE) or a nonword (e.g., YJO). Facilitation of target words related to the concept (JOY) relative to control words (JOE) indicates activation of the target concept.

In short, the present research examines the convergent validity of two evaluative implicit measures, and compares them to a nonevaluative implicit measure in their relation to explicit attitudes and behavioral intentions. The research thus had three key goals. The first was to determine whether implicit and explicit attitudes would in fact converge for neutral targets. If this were the case, the evaluative measures would be associated with liking, and lexical decision performance would be associated with explicit belief in the product benefit and with explicit emotional experience. The second aim was to examine the interrelations of the three implicit measures; the two evaluative measures should be associated with each other, but not necessarily related to the LDT. Finally, we compared the predictive validity of the three implicit attitude measures and the explicit measures in predicting behavioral intentions related to the consumer judgment.

## Methods

Ninety-seven female employees of a consumer goods company participated in a computer-based study. Participants saw images of packages for three different consumer goods

© 2010 Hogrefe Publishing

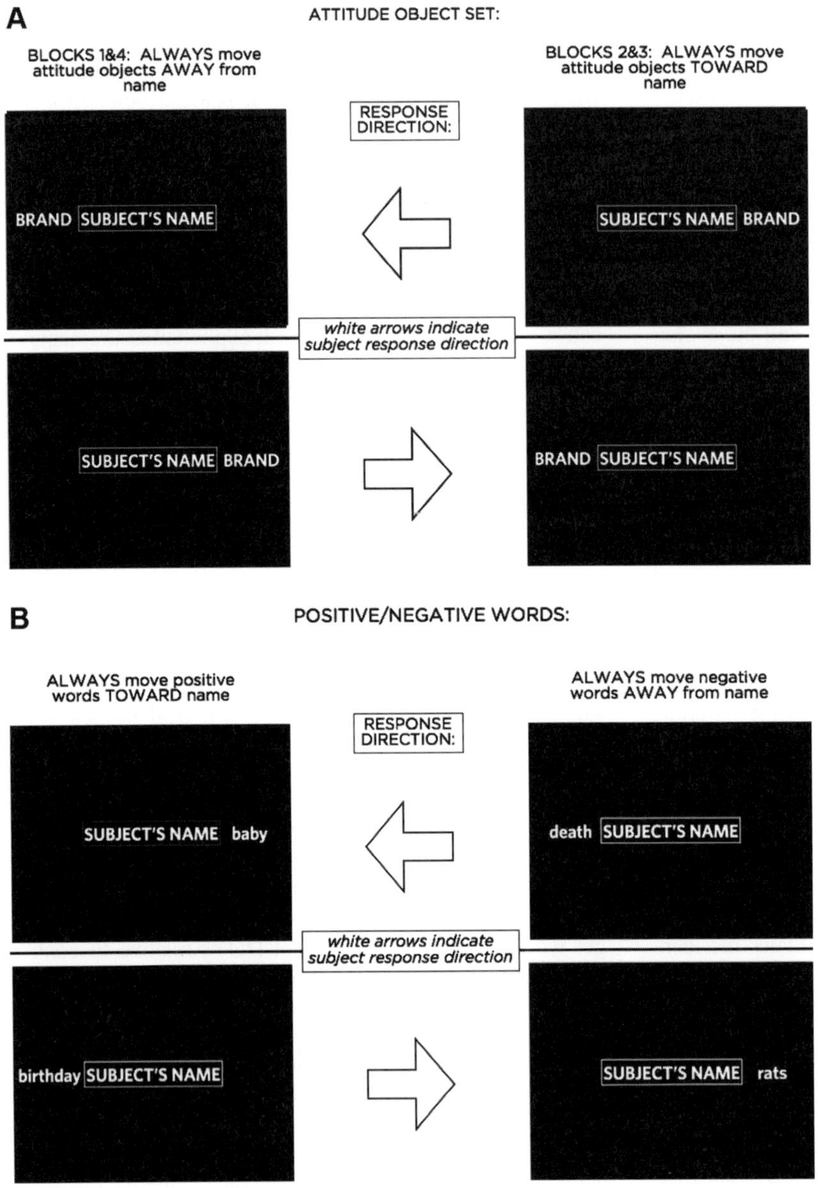


*Figure 1.* Correct response directions for positive and negative words (1a) and attitude objects (1b). The directions "left" and "right" are indicated by the subject by using the keyboard letters "Q" and "P," respectively. The direction refers to the movement of the word or attitude object, not the subject's name, which remained fixed at the center of the screen.

brands (a detergent, a fabric softener, and a cold medicine) presented on a computer monitor. Although these brands were products of the company employing the participants, none of the participants worked in the divisions of the company that produced these products. Participants saw a slide before each new product identifying the product type (e.g., "The next product you will see is a fabric softener"). The order of the packages was counterbalanced. Following the presentation of the three packages, participants completed an LDT, an EVP, and an EMA, all presented using DirectRT software (Empirisoft, 2008).

In the LDT, participants were presented with letter strings that were either words related to the target emotional benefit for each of the three brands (detergent: joy; softener: confidence; and cold medicine: restoration), unrelated words, or nonword letter strings. Nonemotion-related control words were matched for length, frequency in usage, and response time using data from the English Lexicon Project (Balota et al., 2007); nonwords were matched for length and first letter. Participants were instructed to use the "Q" key to indicate if the letter string on the screen was a real word and "P" to indicate if it was not a real word in English. To keep participants oriented, "WORD" and "NOT A WORD" appeared in yellow at the bottom of the screen at the left and right, respectively. Approximately 10 target words appeared for each brand, with an equal number of matched control and nonwords. Mean response latencies were computed for the three string types (target, control, and nonword); the facilitation of the target emotional concept was calculated by subtracting the response latency for

 © 2010 Hogrefe Publishing

the target words from the response latency for the matched control words.[1]

The EVP followed a modified version of the procedures of Fazio et al. (1995). Positive and negative words were preceded by an image related to the brand (i.e., a logo or a package) or a conceptually related control image (e.g., for the cough medicine, a box of tissues or a thermometer). Each image appeared onscreen for 315 ms and was followed by a blank screen for 135 ms. Participants were told that the image was a warning signal to orient their attention and that they did not need to respond to it, but instead should determine as quickly as possible whether the word that then appeared was positive or negative.[2] A positive or negative word then appeared onscreen; participants were instructed to determine whether the word meant "good" or "bad" and to press the "Q" key to indicate that the word meant "good," and the "P" key to indicate that it meant "bad." The words "GOOD" and "BAD" appeared in yellow at the bottom of the screen at the right and left, respectively, to keep participants oriented. Each brand appeared eight times preceding a positive word and eight times preceding a negative word; the order of words and images was randomized. Response times for target images followed by positive words and for target images followed by negative words were calculated as indicators of measures of implicit positivity and implicit negativity, respectively.

In the EMA, following the procedures of Brendl, Markman et al. (2005), participants entered their first name, which appeared in a box in the middle of the screen (see Figure 1 for a schematic). Words appeared either to the left or to the right of their name, about half the distance between the center and edge of the screen. Participants were told to move negative words (e.g., divorce and death) away from their name and positive words (e.g., birthday and baby) toward their name (see Figure 1b). Participants were told that the "Q" key would move objects toward the left and the "P" key would move them toward the right. Thus, the "Q" key would move a word that appeared to the right of the name *toward* the name at the center, and move a word that appeared to the left of the name *away* from the name and off the screen, and the "P" key would do the converse. After a practice block of just positive and negative distractors (e.g., death and baby), they were told that the brand names of the three products they had seen at the start of the session would appear in capitalized font. For the first and fourth experimental blocks, they were told to move these words away from their name, while continuing to move positive words toward their name and negative words away from their name. In the second and third experimental blocks, they were told to move these words toward their name, while continuing to move positive words toward their name and negative words away from their name (see Figure 1a). Each brand name appeared seven times per block; the order of words within each block was randomized. Mean latencies for moving each brand name toward their name (i.e., positivity) and away from their name (i.e., negativity) were calculated.

Following the implicit tasks, participants completed explicit measures of their emotional state, attitude toward the brands, beliefs about the brands' emotional benefits, and purchase intentions. Participants were instructed to use the 1–5 number keys to respond to Likert scale items (where 1 corresponded to the most favorable rating and 5 the least). Participants first rated their explicit emotional state for each of the three target emotions "Right now, I feel (JOYFUL/CONFIDENT/RESTORED)." The order of these items was randomized. One of the three brands' logos then appeared onscreen, and participants completed several ratings for this brand. Scale items appeared below the logo, which remained onscreen for all ratings. Participants rated each brand on their purchase intention (How likely are you to buy this product?), their explicit evaluation of the product (How much do you like this project?), and their belief in the target's emotional benefit "Do you believe this product will make you more (JOYFUL/CONFIDENT/RESTORED)?". After participants had made these ratings for one brand, the next logo would appear and the participants would make the same ratings for that brand, and then for the third brand. The order of the three explicit rating items was randomized within each brand, and the three brands were randomly ordered.

## Results

Incorrect responses for each task (e.g., calling a word a nonword, identifying a positive word as negative, and moving

[1] The implementation and analysis of the LDT used in the present research differed in aim than traditional uses of the LDT. Typically, performance on an LDT is measured for a group exposed to a stimulus prime compared to a control prime, in order to determine whether the stimulus increases activation of a target concept (Meyer & Schvaneveldt, 1971). In the present research, however, we were concerned with the extent to which the activation of different target concepts would (or would not) covary with other implicit measures and with explicit consumer preference measures. That is, instead of the typical research question addressed by an LDT (Does stimulus X increase the accessibility of concept Y?), which would require a comparison of the stimulus condition to a control condition, we posed the research question of whether the general accessibility of a target concept was associated with other measures of interest, which can be addressed correlationally.

[2] These instructions depart from the original instructions of Fazio et al. (1995), in which participants were told that the faces were part of a memory task and that they would later have to identify if they had seen the face previously. Because of the number of tests that participants performed, and the fact that we were testing three attitude objects, we were hesitant to add an additional cognitive burden, and so simply asked participants to orient their attention to the image. Given that neither the original nor our set of instructions included any suggestion of association between the image and the target judgment, and that the priming effect should be automatic and thus independent of any instructions about processing the image, we believe that our nonstandard instructions do not pose any issue in the interpretation of these results. Likewise, we did not include a baseline measure of response latencies to the positive and negative words due to concerns about participant fatigue. We believe that our use of multilevel analytic techniques offers a similar reduction in error variance such a baseline might have likewise provided.

© 2010 Hogrefe Publishing

*Table 1*. Results of implicit measures as predictors of explicit measures

| | EMA negative | EMA positive | EVP negative | EVP positive | LDT |
|---|---|---|---|---|---|
| Liking | $\rho = -0.02$<br>$t(96) = 0.08$<br>$p = .94$ | $\rho = 0.07$<br>$t(96) = 0.26$<br>$p = .80$ | $\rho = 0.22$<br>$t(96) = 0.79$<br>$p = .43$ | $\rho = -0.07$<br>$t(96) = 0.21$<br>$p = .84$ | $\rho = -0.02$<br>$t(96) = 0.05$<br>$p = .96$ |
| Belief in benefit | $\rho = -0.03$<br>$t(96) = 0.08$<br>$p = .94$ | $\rho = -0.31$<br>$t(96) = 0.84$<br>$p = .40$ | $\rho = -0.55$<br>$t(96) = 1.65$<br>$p = .10$ | $\rho = 0.15$<br>$t(96) = 0.32$<br>$p = .62$ | $\rho = -0.50$<br>$t(96) = 1.10$<br>$p = .27$ |
| Explicit emotion | $\rho = -0.43$<br>$t(96) = 1.63$<br>$p = .11$ | $\rho = -0.39$<br>$t(96) = 1.38$<br>$p = .17$ | $\rho = 0.04$<br>$t(96) = 0.12$<br>$p = .91$ | $\rho = 0.25$<br>$t(96) = 0.67$<br>$p = .51$ | **$\rho = -1.04$**<br>**$t(96) = 2.41$**<br>**$p = .02$** |
| Purchase intention | $\rho = -0.07$<br>$t(96) = 0.21$<br>$p = .84$ | $\rho = -0.32$<br>$t(96) = 1.02$<br>$p = .31$ | $\rho = -0.12$<br>$t(96) = 0.35$<br>$p = .73$ | $\rho = -0.19$<br>$t(96) = 0.49$<br>$p = .63$ | **$\rho = -1.34$**<br>**$t(96) = 3.20$**<br>**$p = .002$** |

*Note*. $\rho$ denotes the unstandardized regression coefficient from the hierarchical linear regression, with corresponding $t$ test and $p$ value. Significant cells are shown in bold.

the brand away from the name in a block in which they were instructed to move the word toward the name) were discarded from further analysis. To restore normality, response times were log transformed, and responses more than three standard deviations greater than the within-participant mean for the response type within each task were deleted. As measures were collected for each of three unrelated brands, data were analyzed in hierarchical linear regressions, nesting brands within participants, which helps reduce error variance and improve reliability over the use of a single target.

Both the EMA and EVP allow the calculation of independent scores for positivity (response time to moving the attitude object toward one's name in EMA and to positive words preceded by the attitude object prime in EVP) and negativity (response time to moving the attitude object away from one's name in EMA and to negative words preceded by the attitude object prime in EVP). As predicted, these dimensions were significantly associated across these two measures: For positivity, $\rho = 0.20$, $t(96) = 3.31$, $p = .002$, and for negativity, $\rho = 0.20$, $t(96) = 4.31$, $p < .001$.[3]

In all analyses reported below, the implicit measure was entered as a univariate predictor of the measure of interest in a hierarchical linear regression. In order to reduce possible effects of multicolinearity between the two subfactors, which might mask real significant effects of the subfactors, we treated them as univariate predictors in a hierarchical regression, rather than including both in a multivariate analysis.

Both EMA positivity and both factors of the EVP were unassociated with activation of the target emotion as measured by the LDT, suggesting that their association with each other was not simply an artifact of common method variance. (EMA negativity, $\rho = -0.02$, $t(96) = 0.49$, $p = .63$; EVP negativity, $\rho = -0.07$, $t(96) = -\ 1.03$, $p = .31$; and EVP positivity $\rho = 0.01$, $t(96) = 0.12$, $p = .90$). The EMA positivity measure was significantly associated with the LDT ($\rho = -0.12$, $t(96) = 2.39$, $p = .02$).

If explicit and implicit attitudes converge, we would expect that EMA and EVP would be associated with explicit liking, whereas the LDT would be associated with explicit belief in the product's emotional benefit and/or explicit emotional experience. In fact, none of the implicit measures were associated with explicit liking (see Table 1 for results of all analyses). Likewise, none of the implicit measures were significantly associated with explicit belief in the product benefit, though EVP negativity was marginally associated with belief in the rated benefit, indicating that as negativity was inhibited following a target brand prime, participants showed an increased endorsement of the product's target brand's emotional benefit. However, as predicted, LDT, though not EMA or EVP, was significantly associated with the measure of explicit emotional experience associated with the brand (Right now, I feel...).

In the context of consumer evaluations, the most critical explicit assessment is the behavioral intention to purchase the product. As might be expected from the lack of relationship with explicit liking, neither EMA nor EVP was significantly associated with purchase intention. However, LDT was significantly associated with purchase intention, such that facilitation of the brand's emotional attribute was associated with increased intention to purchase the product. This effect remained significant when explicit emotional experience was included as a predictor of purchase intention, $r = -1.33$, $t(96) = 3.19$, $p = .002$, suggesting that the effect of implicit activation on purchase intention was not mediated by explicit emotion.

## Discussion

The results of this examination of three implicit measures are highly informative. The two evaluative measures, evalu-

[3] Fazio et al. (1995) used the EVP as both a bivariate and aggregate measure. No results where the EVP subscores were nonsignificant predictors were significant if the aggregated EVP was used instead.

 © 2010 Hogrefe Publishing

ative movement assessment (EMA) and evaluative priming (EVP), were correlated for both negative and positive associations. It is perhaps surprising that implicit activation of product benefits, as measured by the lexical decision task (LDT), was associated with positive implicit evaluations of the product on only EMA but not EVP. However, the evaluative tasks differed in how the attitude object was presented. In EMA, the brand name appeared onscreen and remained until the participant made a response. In contrast, in evaluative priming, the brand was represented by an image that appeared onscreen for less than half a second. Moreover, in order to avoid repetition of the same package image, which might create a confound in evaluations due to valence effects of enhanced fluency (Bornstein, 1989; Janiszewski, 1993), we used both images of the full package and close-up images of package details as primes. It is therefore plausible that EVP, as presently instantiated, was less robust than the EMA, which might explain why EVP, but not EMA, failed to correlate with the LDT.

The second goal of this research was to examine the convergence or divergence of these measures from explicit measures in a naturalistic attitude context. Even in a consumer context, in which individuals have a low motivation to misrepresent attitudes, we found divergence of explicit and implicit evaluations. Though it is possible that explicit evaluations were subject to social desirability pressures (participants were employees of the corporation that manufactured the target products, but worked in unrelated divisions and were tested outside their workspace by unknown experimenters), there should still be substantially less pressure to alter responses about detergent preference relative to pressures to conceal prejudiced attitudes. Thus, the present research strongly suggests that divergence may be a common rather than rare feature of implicit and explicit attitudes (Hofmann et al., 2005; Nosek, 2005). It is possible, however, that despite the use of multilevel modeling techniques, there was still excessive error variance in our implicit measures. We did not include a neutral-prime baseline measure as in Fazio et al.'s (1995) original EVP, and in the EMA, participants might have used the surface cue of the brand names appearing in capitalized font rather than deeply evaluating the targets. Further replications of a pattern of divergence in these naturally formed attitudes would more strongly support this conclusion. Overall, this result, taken with previous laboratory studies, undermines the idea that implicit and explicit attitudes are drawn from the same basic attitude representation (Fazio & Olson, 2003; Petty & Wegener, 1998).

The final goal of the research, to compare the predictive validity of the three implicit attitude measures for behavioral intentions, found that the divergence of implicit evaluations from explicit measures extended to these behavioral intentions as well, as neither EMA nor EVP predicted purchase intention. However, implicit activation of the product benefit, as measured by LDT, did significantly predict behavioral intention. There are at least three possible ways of conceptualizing the LDT, with each conceptualization suggesting a different interpretation of this correlation. One interpretation is that activation of product benefits, as measured by the LDT, represents a cognitive (as opposed to affective or evaluative) component of the implicit attitude. The lack of a correlation with explicit beliefs about the product would thus parallel the lack of correlation between implicit and explicit evaluations. However, this interpretation would imply that the cognitive, but not evaluative, component of an implicit attitude predicts purchase intention, which seems dubious in light of past research on implicit evaluations and behavior (Dovidio et al., 2002; McConnell & Leibold, 2001; Wilson et al., 2000). For this reason, we find this interpretation the least palatable. Another interpretation, supported by the correlation between the LDT and explicit emotional experience, is that the LDT measured an implicit emotional state. Although LDT and explicit emotion were correlated, the LDT predicted unshared variance in purchase intention, suggesting that these levels of emotional experience, like the two levels of evaluation, can diverge. This interpretation would suggest that "gut feelings" are useful predictors of consumer preferences (see also Maison, Greenwald, & Bruin, 2004). A third interpretation is that the accessibility of the target emotions in the LDT reflects the activation of nonconscious goals (cf. Aarts, Dijksterhuis, & de Vries, 2001), which have received a tremendous amount of attention in the consumer literature (Bargh, 2002; Dijksterhuis et al., 2005). Priming a goal leads to increases in the effort expended on achieving that goal (Bargh, Gollwitzer, Lee-Chai, Barndollar, & Troetschel, 2001), increases positive appraisals of objects that can help with goal progress (Ferguson & Bargh, 2004), and leads to devaluation of objects unrelated to active goals (Brendl, Markman, & Messner, 2003). If the LDT reflects the degree of nonconscious activation of emotional-state goals, the association between the LDT and purchase intention would thus result from active emotional goals (e.g., to be joyful) leading to increased preference for products that could help satisfy that goal (e.g., a detergent associated with joyfulness). The nonconscious goal literature has demonstrated that goal activation (e.g., thirst) is a necessary condition for other variables to have a behavioral effect (e.g., to be able to alter beverage consumption; Berridge & Winkielman, 2003). This interpretation of the LDT as an indicator of active nonconscious goals might explain why it, and not global measures of implicit attitude, was associated with purchase intention, as the LDT (and not the evaluative measures) would measure this necessary state of goal activation. Clearly, all three of these interpretations are speculative and would require experimental evidence to be disentangled. Likewise, it remains to be seen whether implicit evaluations or emotional benefit activation predicts actual purchase behavior, rather than ratings of purchase intentions.

In short, the present research offers valuable insights into how implicit measures of consumer attitudes relate to each other, explicit attitudes, and behavioral intentions to purchase the product. These results are not merely informative about methodological concerns in consumer research, but also speak to the structure of attitudes within the consumer-goods context, and thus are important within both the attitudes and the consumer decision-making literatures.

© 2010 Hogrefe Publishing

## Acknowledgments

We wish to thank Allen McConnell for his comments on an earlier version of this manuscript, and Sara Austin and Amanda Trask for their editing assistance.


## References


Aarts, H., Dijksterhuis, A., & de Vries, P. J. (2001). On the psychology of drinking: Being thirsty and perceptually ready. *British Journal of Psychology, 92*, 631–642.

Balota, D. A., Yap, M. J., Cortese, M. J., Hutchison, K. A., Kessler, B., Loftis, B., et al. (2007). *The English Lexicon project. Behavior research methods, 39*, 445–459. Available from http://elexicon.wustl.edu/.

Bargh, J. A. (2002). Losing consciousness: Automatic influences on consumer judgment, behavior, and motivation. *Journal of Consumer Research, 29*, 280–285.

Bargh, J. A., Chaiken, S., Govender, R., & Pratto, F. (1992). The generality of the automatic attitude activation effect. *Journal of Personality and Social Psychology, 62*, 893–912.

Bargh, J. A., Gollwitzer, P. M., Lee-Chai, A., Barndollar, K., & Troetschel, R. (2001). The automated will: Nonconscious activation and pursuit of behavioral goals. *Journal of Personality and Social Psychology, 81*, 1014–1027.

Berridge, K., & Winkielman, P. (2003). What is an unconscious emotion? (The case for unconscious "liking"). *Cognition and Emotion, 17*, 181–211.

Bornstein, R. F. (1989). Exposure and affect: Overview and meta-analysis of research 1968–1987. *Psychological Bulletin, 106*, 265–289.

Brendl, C. M., Chattopadhyay, A., Pelham, B. W., & Carvallo, M. (2005). Name letter branding: Valence transfers when product specific needs are active. *Journal of Consumer Research, 32*, 405–415.

Brendl, C. M., Markman, A. B., & Messner, C. (2003). The devaluation effect: Activating a need devalues unrelated objects. *Journal of Consumer Research, 29*, 463–473.

Brendl, C. M., Markman, A. B., & Messner, C. (2005). Indirectly measuring evaluations of several attitude objects in relation to a neutral reference point. *Journal of Experimental Social Psychology, 41*, 346–368.

Cacioppo, J. T., & Berntson, G. G. (1994). Relationship between attitudes and evaluative space: A critical review, with emphasis on the separability of positive and negative substrates. *Psychological Bulletin, 115*, 401–423.

Chartrand, T. L. (2005). The role of conscious awareness in consumer behavior. *Journal of Consumer Psychology, 15*, 203–210.

Chen, M., & Bargh, J. (1999). Consequences of automatic evaluation: Immediate behavioral predispositions to approach or avoid the stimulus. *Personality and Social Psychology Bulletin, 25*, 215–224.

DeCoster, J., Banner, M. J., Smith, E. R., & Semin, G. R. (2006). On the inexplicity of the implicit: Differences in the information provided by implicit and explicit tests. *Social Cognition, 24*, 5–21.

Dijksterhuis, A., Smith, P. K., vanBaaren, R. B., & Wigboldus, D. H. J. (2005). The unconscious consumer: Effects of environment on consumer behavior. *Journal of Consumer Psychology, 15*, 193–202.

Dovidio, J. F., Kawakami, K., & Gaertner, S. L. (2002). Implicit and explicit prejudice and interracial interaction. *Journal of Personality and Social Psychology, 82*, 62–68.

Empirisoft (2008). *DirectRT (v2008) [computer software]*. New York: Empirisoft.

Fazio, R. H., Jackson, J. R., Dunton, B. C., & Williams, C. J. (1995). Variability in automatic activation as an unobtrusive measure of racial attitudes: A bona fide pipeline? *Journal of Personality and Social Psychology, 69*, 1013–1027.

Fazio, R. H., & Olson, M. A. (2003). Implicit measures in social cognition research: Their meaning and uses. *Annual Review of Psychology, 54*, 297–327.

Fazio, R. H., Sanbonmatsu, D. M., Powell, M. C., & Kardes, F. R. (1986). On the automatic activation of attitudes. *Journal of Personality and Social Psychology, 50*, 229–238.

Ferguson, M. J., & Bargh, J. A. (2004). Liking is for doing: The effects of goal pursuit on automatic evaluation. *Journal of Personality and Social Psychology, 87*, 557–572.

Ferraro, R., Bettman, J. R., & Chartrand, T. L. (2009). The power of strangers: The effect of incidental consumer brand encounters on brand choice. *Journal of Consumer Research, 35*, 729–741.

Greenwald, A. G., McGhee, D. E., & Schwartz, J. L. K. (1998). Measuring individual differences in implicit cognition: The Implicit Association Test. *Journal of Personality and Social Psychology, 74*, 1464–1480.

Hofmann, W., Gawronski, B., Gschwendner, T., Le, H., & Schmitt, M. (2005). A meta-analysis on the correlation between the Implicit Association Test and explicit self-report measures. *Personality and Social Psychology Bulletin, 31*, 1369–1385.

Hogendoorn, S., Wolters, L. H., Vervoort, L., Prins, P., Boer, F., & de Haan, E. (2008). An indirect and direct measure of anxiety-related perceived control in children: The Implicit Association Procedure (IAP) and Anxiety Control Questionnaire for Children (ACQ-C). *Journal of Behavior Therapy and Experimental Psychiatry, 39*, 436–450.

Janiszewski, C. (1993). Preattentive mere exposure effects. *Journal of Consumer Research, 20*, 376–392.

Maison, D., Greenwald, A. G., & Bruin, R. H. (2004). Predictive validity of the Implicit Association Test in studies of brands, consumer attitudes, and behavior. *Journal of Consumer Psychology, 14*, 405–415.

Markman, A., & Brendl, C. M. (2005). Constraining theories of embodied cognition. *Psychological Science, 16*, 6–10.

McConnell, A. R., & Leibold, J. M. (2001). Relations among the Implicit Association Test, discriminatory behavior, and explicit measures of racial attitudes. *Journal of Experimental Social Psychology, 37*, 435–442.

Meyer, D. E., & Schvaneveldt, R. W. (1971). Facilitation in recognizing pairs of words: Evidence of a dependence between retrieval operations. *Journal of Experimental Psychology, 90*, 227–234.

Nosek, B. A. (2005). Moderators of the relationship between implicit and explicit evaluation. *Journal of Experimental Psychology: General, 134*, 565–584.

Petty, R. E., & Wegener, D. T. (1998). Attitude change: Multiple roles for persuasion variables. In D. T. Gilbert, S. T. Fiske, & G. Lindzey (Eds.), *Handbook of social psychology* (4th ed., Vol. 1, pp. 323–390). New York: McGraw-Hill.

Reinecke, A., Becker, E. S., & Rinck, M. (2010). Test-retest reliability and validity of three indirect tasks assessing implicit threat associations and behavioural response tendencies. *Zeitschrift für psychologie / Journal of Psychology, 218*, 4–11.

Rinck, M., & Becker, E. S. (2007). Approach and avoidance in fear of spiders. *Journal of Behavior Therapy and Experimental Psychiatry, 38*, 105–120.

Rotteveel, M., & Phaf, R. H. (2004). Automatic affective evaluation does not automatically predispose for arm flexion and extension. *Emotion, 4*, 156–172.


 © 2010 Hogrefe Publishing

Rydell, R. J., & McConnell, A. R. (2006). Understanding implicit and explicit attitude change: A systems of reasoning analysis. *Journal of Personality and Social Psychology, 91*, 995–1008.

Rydell, R. J., McConnell, A. R., Mackie, D. M., & Strain, L. M. (2006). Of two minds: Forming and changing valence-inconsistent implicit attitudes. *Psychological Science, 17*, 954–958.

Schnabel, K., Banse, R., & Asendorpf, J. (2006). Employing automatic approach and avoidance tendencies for the assessment of implicit personality self-concept: The Implicit Association Procedure (IAP). *Experimental Psychology, 53*, 69–76.

Seibt, B., Neumann, R., Nussinson, R., & Strack, F. (2008). Movement direction or change in distance? Self and object related approach-avoidance motions. *Journal of Experimental Social Psychology, 44*, 713–720.

van Dantzig, S., Pecher, D., & Zwaan, R. A. (2008). Approach and avoidance as action effects. *Quarterly Journal of Experimental Psychology, 61*, 1298–1306.

van Dantzig, S., Zeelenberg, R., & Pecher, D. (2009). Unconstraining theories of embodied cognition. *Journal of Experimental Social Psychology, 45*, 345–351.

Wentura, D., Rothermund, D., & Bak, P. (2000). Automatic vigilance: The attention-grabbing power of approach and avoidance-related social information. *Journal of Personality and Social Psychology, 78*, 1024–1037.

Wilson, T. D., Lindsey, S., & Schooler, T. Y. (2000). A model of dual attitudes. *Psychological Review, 107*, 101–126.

Amy Summerville

Department of Psychology
Miami University
222 Psychology Building
90 N. Patterson Avenue
Oxford, OH 45056
USA
Tel. +1 513 529-6126
Fax +1 513 529-2420
E-mail summera@muohio.edu

© 2010 Hogrefe Publishing 

Original Article

# Using Community Data to Test the Discriminant Validity of Ethnic/ Racial Group IATs

Irene V. Blair,[1] Charles M. Judd,[1] Edward P. Havranek,[2] and John F. Steiner[3]

[1]University of Colorado at Boulder, USA
[2]Denver Health Medical Center, USA
[3]Institute for Health Research, Kaiser Permanente Colorado, USA

**Abstract.** The present study used a multi-method, multi-measure, multi-group approach to investigate the discriminant validity of prejudice-related Implicit Association Tests (IATs). Community members from three ethnic/racial groups in the US completed IATs and explicit measures of attitudes toward African Americans and Latinos, with Whites used as the comparison group. The results of this study provided strong support for the discriminant validity of the IATs by showing, (a) expected patterns of variation among the three participant groups that were unique to each IAT, (b) unique relations between responses on each IAT and corresponding (same-group) explicit measures of prejudice, and (c) invariance across the three participant groups in the degree to which the attitude measures loaded on two latent factors, indicating distinct attitudes toward African Americans and Latinos.

**Keywords:** Implicit Association Test, ethnic, prejudice, African American, Latino

The Implicit Association Test (IAT; Greenwald, McGhee, & Schwartz, 1998) has garnered tremendous attention since its introduction 10 years ago, especially with regard to its measurement of individual differences in implicit group attitudes (Nosek, Greenwald, & Banaji, 2005, 2007). Respondents on the IAT are asked to categorize stimuli into one of four superordinate categories, representing two concept dimensions (e.g., *racial groups*: Black vs. White and *evaluation*: good vs. bad). The strength of an individual respondent's association between concepts is determined by his or her speed in correctly categorizing the stimuli under two different sorting conditions. Most White Americans, for example, are significantly faster to complete the task when the stimuli representing the "Black" and "bad" categories require the same response (e.g., left key press) and the stimuli representing the "White" and "good" categories require another response (e.g., right key press), compared to when "Black" and "good" responses are the same and "White" and "bad" responses are the same, indicating an implicit preference for White Americans over Black Americans (Nosek, Banaji, & Greenwald, 2002; Nosek et al., 2005).

The IAT has arguably become the dominant measure of implicit attitudes due to its robust effects, ease of administration, reliability, and predictive validity (see Lane, Banaji, Nosek, & Greenwald, 2007; Nosek et al., 2007). In the intergroup domain specifically, the measure has had success in predicting a variety of relevant judgments and behaviors, including judgments of individual minority group members, nonverbal behavior during intergroup interactions, preference for a White task partner over a Black partner, and reports of racial discrimination including verbal slurs and physical harm (see Greenwald, Poehlman, Uhlmann, & Banaji, 2009).

## The Discriminant Validity of the IAT

Notwithstanding its successes, the IAT has been criticized on the degree to which it measures associations (e.g., White+good) or other cognitive processes that may be related to both task performance and biased judgments. For example, individual differences in the costs of task switching (Mierke & Klauer, 2001) or in reliance on figure-ground asymmetries (Rothermund & Wentura, 2001) could influence both performance on the IAT and biased group judgments (Gawronski, 2002). As such, the IAT might not be measuring an individual's implicit attitude toward a specific group but rather a more general process that could underlie a number of different "attitudes." Although the IAT may have good reliability and predictive validity, it could still have poor *discriminant validity* in terms of what it is measuring.

Contributing to this potential problem is the IAT's reliance on comparative judgments to complete the tasks: Black versus White, male versus female, elderly versus young adult, etc. These built-in comparisons mean that results from


DOI: 10.1027/0044-3409/a000006
© 2010 Hogrefe Publishing

a specific IAT could be interpreted with regard to either or both groups. For example, being faster to categorize White+good than Black+good may indicate a pro-White attitude, an anti-Black attitude, or some combination of the two. In many situations such a distinction is unimportant and the IAT will still produce valid predictions, such as the prediction of a White applicant being hired over a Black applicant, whether the underlying sentiment is pro-White or anti-Black. However, since one dominant group is typically contrasted with a variety of minority groups (e.g., Whites in the US compared with other ethnic/racial groups), it is important to determine whether a particular ethnic/racial IAT reveals an attitude that is specific to the minority group of interest or a general pro-White attitude.

To our knowledge, only one study has investigated this issue. Gawronski (2002) administered two group IATs (German:Asian and German:Turkish) and measures of explicit attitudes to a sample of German participants. The results revealed relatively modest correlations between the two IATs and between each IAT and its respective (same-group) explicit prejudice measure ($r \approx .30$), consistent with the hypothesis that the attitude estimates would be related but not redundant. Structural equation modeling further revealed significant relations between each IAT and the same-group explicit prejudice measure, and simultaneously, that the cross paths between implicit and explicit attitudes toward different groups were not significant.

Gawronski's results provide support for the discriminant validity of the IAT, but a more comprehensive analysis would demonstrate patterns of discriminant validity that are consistent with expected variations among different participant groups. Thus, the goal of the present study was to examine the discriminant validity of the IAT, using data collected from a diverse sample of community members. We recruited African American, Latino, and White community members to complete IATs and explicit attitude measures toward African Americans (Blacks) and Latinos, compared with Whites. We then examined whether the patterns of responses indicated distinct attitudes toward Blacks and Latinos.

## Hypotheses

1. As shown in prior research on attitudes toward high-status versus low-status groups (see Jost, Banaji, & Nosek, 2004), the IATs are expected to reveal overall pro-White attitudes. However, the degree to which this is true is expected to differ by participants' ethnic/racial group and IAT.

1A. Black:White IAT: African American participants ought to show significantly less pro-White bias than White participants. We expect that additionally, the Latino participants will also demonstrate less pro-White bias than White participants, but more bias than the African American participants, since Latinos will not be responding to their ingroup on this IAT and White Americans will tend to be favored as the high-status group.

1B. Latino:White IAT: Latino participants are expected to show significantly less pro-White bias than White participants, and this time the African American participants are expected to demonstrate a level of bias that is in-between the other two groups since on this IAT they will not be responding to their ingroup.

2. Implicit attitudes revealed by each IAT are expected to predict explicit attitudes toward the same groups, even after shared method variance is controlled.

2A. Attitudes on the Black:White IAT ought to predict explicit attitudes toward Blacks but not explicit attitudes toward Latinos (vs. Whites), controlling for method variance.

2B. Attitudes on the Latino:White IAT ought to predict explicit attitudes toward Latinos but not explicit attitudes toward Blacks (vs. Whites), controlling for method variance.

3. Another way to state 2A and 2B is in terms of multi-group confirmatory factor analysis, which has the added advantage of testing for participant group differences in these effects.

3A. This analysis is expected to support a two-factor latent-variable model in which implicit and explicit attitudes toward Blacks uniquely load on a "Black attitude" factor that is distinct from a second "Latino attitude" factor, with implicit and explicit attitudes toward Latinos uniquely loading on the latter.

3B. The above-specified model is expected to hold for each of the three participant groups, although the groups ought to differ in their means and possibly their variances.

# Methods

To obtain a broad sample of community members, participants were recruited from five patient waiting areas within Denver Health, the urban healthcare system serving a disadvantaged, ethnically/racially diverse population in the Denver metropolitan area. Participants completed the study measures on portable Macintosh computers, in either English or Spanish as desired, in return for a $20 gift card.[1] The protocol for this study was approved by the Colorado Multiple Institutional Review Board.

Of the 284 individuals who consented to participate, the data from 43 were dropped for the following reasons: four participants were unable to complete the tasks due to illiter-

[1] We are most grateful to Gwynn Brownell, Claudia Cespedes, and Inez Smith for their help with this study.

© 2010 Hogrefe Publishing 

acy or other physical/cognitive problems; 13 participants had computer problems (e.g., power failures); seven participants responded too quickly for valid measures (see Greenwald, Nosek, & Banaji, 2003); and 19 participants did not self-identify with one of the focal ethnic/racial participant groups. For the remaining 241 participants, the average age category was 36–45 years old, the average family income category was $16,000–$35,000, and the average education category was just above high school; 63% were women; 38% were Latino, 34% were White, and 28% were African American.

## Study Measures

### IAT Measures of Implicit Ethnic/Racial Attitudes

Each participant completed the measures self-paced, beginning with 13 blocks of IAT trials. The first seven blocks were designed to assess implicit attitudes toward Latinos versus Whites, with an initial 2 blocks of 20 single-category trials (positive vs. negative and White vs. Latino), 2 blocks of 20 then 40 "consistent" dual-category trials (White+positive vs. Latino+negative), 1 block of 40 switched single-category trials (Latino vs. White), and 2 final blocks of 20 then 40 "inconsistent" dual-category trials (Latino+positive vs. White+negative). Blocks 8–13 used the same block structure to assess implicit attitudes toward Blacks versus Whites, minus the positive versus negative block of single-category trials. The two measures differed only in their face stimuli.

Because the focus of the study was on comparisons among participant groups and the covariances of IAT and explicit attitude measures, all participants received the same order of measures, with the "consistent" blocks of an IAT always appearing before the "inconsistent" blocks. Prior research has shown that this block ordering might result in a small increase in pro-White bias on the IAT (Greenwald & Nosek, 2001). Nosek et al. (2005) demonstrated, however, that giving participants 40 trials to practice sorting the categories that have switched positions, as we did, usually eliminates this order effect. Nonetheless, caution should be used in interpreting the absolute values of the IAT effects produced in this study.

#### IAT Stimuli

The pictures used to represent Latinos, Blacks, and Whites were selected from a publicly accessible website and edited to portray only the face, from hairline to chin and from ear to ear. On the basis of pretesting, 10 Latino, 10 Black, and 10 White photographs were chosen (five male and five female in each group). Across groups, the photographs were matched in perceived age, attractiveness, and agreement on ethnic/racial identity ($M$ = 99% correct identification for all three groups; contact the first author for pretesting details).

The stimuli used to represent the categories good and bad were selected from those commonly used in IAT research and were, respectively, *pleasant, delight, helpful, joy, beautiful, smile, wonderful, enjoy, cheerful*, and *success; horrible, angry, terrible, tragic, hate, destroy, brutal, evil, disaster*, and *ugly*.

#### IAT Scoring

Scores from each IAT were calculated for each participant, using the $d$ score method advised by Greenwald et al. (2003). The internal reliability of the Latino:White IAT was $\alpha = .76$, and the reliability of the Black:White IAT was $\alpha = .60$.

### Measures of Explicit Ethnic/Racial Attitudes

Explicit ethnic/racial attitudes were assessed with two measures for each of the three groups of interest: Blacks, Latinos, and Whites. The first measure was the Feeling Thermometer Scale, on which participants were asked to type in a number for each ethnic/racial group using a 0–100° scale to describe how warmly or coolly they feel toward the group. The second measure was a set of three semantic differential scales, on which participants were asked to rate each group as, "hardworking – lazy," foolish – wise," and "cooperative – hostile." All trait ratings were blocked by target group.

#### Explicit Attitude Scoring

The explicit attitude measures were scored to be as analogous to the IATs as possible. A Black:White thermometer score was calculated by subtracting the warmth rating of Blacks from the warmth rating of Whites, and a Latino: White thermometer score was calculated by subtracting the warmth rating of Latinos from the warmth rating of Whites. The same procedure was followed for the trait ratings, with the additional step of averaging the three difference scores for each trait, for each group: Black:White and Latino:White. The internal reliability of the averaged Latino:White trait-rating scale was $\alpha = .58$, and the reliability of the Black:White trait-rating scale was $\alpha = .61$.

## Results

Table 1 provides descriptive information for all of the attitude measures, overall and by participant group.[2] These statistics were largely consistent with past research: overall

[2] Many analyses reported are based on < 241 cases due to missing data ($N$ for each measure is shown in Table 1). All available data were used in any particular analysis.

 © 2010 Hogrefe Publishing

*Table 1.* Descriptive statistics for the attitude measures, overall and by ethnic/racial group

| Measure, overall by participant group | *N* | Mean | *SD* | Effect size (Cohen's *d*) |
|---|---|---|---|---|
| *IAT – Black:White, overall* | 241 | 0.22 | 0.34 | 1.30 |
| African Americans | 67 | 0.05 | 0.30 | 0.34 |
| Latinos | 91 | 0.21 | 0.36 | 1.20 |
| Whites | 83 | 0.36 | 0.29 | 2.57 |
| *IAT – Latino:White, overall* | 241 | 0.19 | 0.43 | 0.87 |
| African Americans | 67 | 0.13 | 0.36 | 0.74 |
| Latinos | 91 | 0.01 | 0.43 | 0.04 |
| Whites | 83 | 0.43 | 0.38 | 2.26 |
| *Thermometer – Black:White, overall* | 203 | −0.62 | 24.00 | 0.05 |
| African Americans | 53 | −14.49 | 25.28 | 1.16 |
| Latinos | 74 | 0.65 | 19.19 | 0.07 |
| Whites | 76 | 7.83 | 23.23 | 0.68 |
| *Thermometer – Latino:White, overall* | 214 | −1.41 | 23.90 | 0.12 |
| African Americans | 57 | −1.60 | 20.80 | 0.16 |
| Latinos | 77 | −10.13 | 22.98 | 0.89 |
| Whites | 80 | 7.11 | 24.03 | 0.60 |
| *Traits – Black:White, overall* | 232 | −0.01 | 1.46 | 0.01 |
| African Americans | 65 | −0.70 | 1.68 | 0.84 |
| Latinos | 85 | 0.38 | 1.28 | 0.60 |
| Whites | 82 | 0.13 | 1.26 | 0.21 |
| *Traits – Latino:White, overall* | 233 | −0.25 | 1.29 | 0.40 |
| African Americans | 66 | −0.31 | 1.03 | 0.61 |
| Latinos | 85 | −0.47 | 1.25 | 0.75 |
| Whites | 82 | 0.01 | 1.47 | 0.02 |

*Note.* IAT scores are *d* scores, with higher numbers indicating more pro-White bias; thermometer scores are differences in degree ratings, with higher numbers indicating more pro-White bias; trait scores are differences in scale ratings, with higher numbers indicating more pro-White bias.

pro-White biases in implicit attitudes and little overall explicit bias. Of greater importance at present is the degree to which the two types of attitudes vary and covary according to participants' ethnic/racial group, as an indication of the measures' discriminant validity. These are questions to which we now turn.

## Between-Group Differences on the IAT Measures

As shown in Figure 1 (see also Table 1), there were significant differences among the three ethnic/racial groups in both Black:White IAT scores and Latino:White IAT scores, respectively, $F(2, 238) = 18.03$, $p < .0001$, Cohen's $d = 0.78$, and $F(2, 238) = 25.87$, $p < .0001$, Cohen's $d = 0.93$. As predicted, on the Black:White IAT the Black participants demonstrated the lowest level of bias ($M = 0.05$); the White participants produced the highest level of pro-White bias on this measure ($M = 0.36$), and the Latino participants scored in-between the other two groups ($M = 0.21$). These differences were all statistically significant: Black versus White participants, $F(1, 238) = 36.00, p < .0001$, Cohen's $d = 0.78$, Black versus Latino participants, $F(1, 238) = 10.18, p < .01$, Cohen's $d = 0.41$, and Latino versus White participants, $F(1, 238) = 9.66, p < .01$, Cohen's $d = 0.40$.

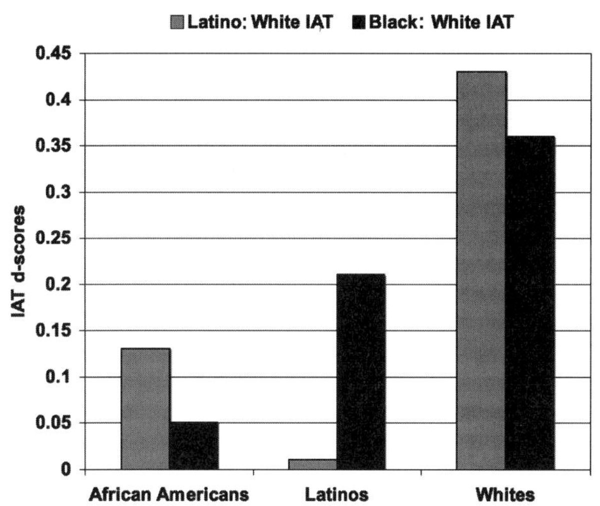


*Figure 1.* Mean scores for the Latino:White and Black: White IAT measures, by ethnic/racial participant groups. Higher numbers indicate greater pro-White bias on the measure.

Results on the Latino:White IAT were analogous: The Latino participants now demonstrated the lowest level of bias on this IAT ($M = 0.01$); the White participants again produced the highest level of pro-White bias ($M = 0.43$); and the Black participants now scored in-between the other two groups ($M = 0.13$). All group differences were again statistically significant: Latino versus White participants, $F(1, 238) = 49.80$, $p < .0001$, Cohen's $d = 0.91$, Latino versus Black participants, $F(1, 238) = 3.72$, $p = .05$, Cohen's $d = 0.25$, and Black versus White participants, $F(1, 238) = 21.44$, $p < .0001$, Cohen's $d = 0.60$.

In support of their discriminant validity, the two IATs produced different yet predictable patterns of results among the three ethnic/racial participant groups. This occurred despite the fact that both IATs relied on the same dominant comparison group (Whites), suggesting that the associations revealed reflect more than a general attitude toward the dominant group.

## Between-Group Differences on the Explicit Attitude Measures

As shown in Table 1, there were also significant differences among the three ethnic/racial groups in explicit attitudes, as shown in Black:White thermometer scores, $F(2, 200) = 15.65$, $p < .0001$, Cohen's $d = 0.79$, Latino:White thermometer scores, $F(2, 211) = 11.19$, $p < .0001$, Cohen's $d = 0.65$, Black:White trait ratings, $F(2, 229) = 11.70$, $p < .0001$, Cohen's $d = 0.64$, and Latino:White trait ratings, $F(2, 230) = 3.03$, $p = .05$, Cohen's $d = 0.32$. Of great interest is the finding that the patterns of explicit attitudes reported by the three ethnic/racial participant groups largely followed those found on the IATs, even though the explicit measures revealed different mean levels of bias than the IATs. On both thermometer measures, the White participants expressed the highest levels of pro-White bias, the participants from the target minority group expressed the least pro-White bias (indeed expressing strong ingroup favoritism), and participants from the "uninvolved" minority group (i.e., Latinos on the Black:White thermometer and African Americans on the Latino:White thermometer) expressed levels of bias that were between the other two groups. Similar but weaker patterns were found with the trait-rating measures. Thus the discriminant validity of the IAT is further supported by the consistency between IAT and explicit measures in predicted patterns of attitudes among the three ethnic/racial groups.

## Relations Between IAT and Explicit Attitude Measures

The bivariate correlations among the IAT and explicit measures of ethnic/racial attitudes showed that, across participants, the Black:White IAT scores were moderately but significantly correlated with Black:White thermometer scores and Black:White trait ratings ($r = .23$ and $r = .24$, respectively). The Latino:White IAT scores were similarly related to the Latino:White thermometer and trait ratings ($r = .26$ and $r = .19$, respectively). There were also, however, significant correlations between measures of Black: White and Latino:White attitudes – for the same type of measure (e.g., Black:White IAT and Latino:White IAT, $r = .40$) and between different types of measures (e.g., Latino:White IAT and Black:White thermometer, $r = .14$).

To examine whether each IAT has a unique relation with explicit attitudes toward the same group, we conducted multivariate regressions in which each explicit attitude measure (e.g., the Black:White thermometer) was simultaneously regressed on both IAT measures. As shown in Table 2, all four regression models showed that once shared variance

*Table 2.* Results of each explicit attitude measure regressed simultaneously on both IAT measures

| Explicit measure ($N$) predictors | Unstandardized parameter estimates | Standard error | $t$ value | Cohen's $d$ |
|---|---|---|---|---|
| *Black:White thermometer (203)* | | | | |
| Intercept | −4.64 | 2.03 | | |
| Latino:White IAT | 2.55 | 4.16 | 0.61 | 0.09 |
| Black:White IAT | 15.19 | 5.47 | 2.78** | 0.39 |
| *Latino:White thermometer (214)* | | | | |
| Intercept | −4.80 | 1.94 | | |
| Latino:White IAT | 13.69 | 4.08 | 3.36*** | 0.46 |
| Black:White IAT | 1.99 | 5.20 | 0.38 | 0.05 |
| *Black:White traits (232)* | | | | |
| Intercept | −0.24 | 0.11 | | |
| Latino:White IAT | −.01 | 0.23 | 0.03 | 0.00 |
| Black:White IAT | 1.02 | 0.30 | 3.41*** | 0.45 |
| *Latino:White traits (233)* | | | | |
| Intercept | −0.43 | 0.10 | | |
| Latino:White IAT | 0.43 | .21 | 2.10* | 0.28 |
| Black:White IAT | 0.39 | 0.26 | 1.51 | 0.20 |

*Note.* $*p < .05$, $**p < .01$, $***p < .001$.

 © 2010 Hogrefe Publishing

between the two IATs was controlled, scores on the explicit attitude measure were significantly predicted by the same-group IAT scores but not by the other-group IAT scores. These results provide further support for the discriminant validity of the IAT in the specific attitude being measured. At the same time, the relations between the implicit and explicit measures, though specific to each group, were moderate enough to demonstrate non-redundancy of constructs (i.e., the Black:White IAT and the Black:White thermometer were not redundant measures of the same construct).

## Confirmatory Factor Analysis

Thus far the discriminant validity of the IAT measures has been demonstrated by predicted patterns of variance among the three ethnic/racial participant groups, and predicted patterns of covariance between IAT and explicit attitude measures for same versus different target groups. Our last analysis of the IATs' discriminant validity used confirmatory factor analysis to explore further the structure of the data in terms of differences in attitudes toward the two minority groups (Black:White vs. Latino:White) and, simultaneously, differences among the three ethnic/racial participant groups. Such an analysis allows us to take full advantage of the multi-method, multi-measure, multi-group nature of our data.

The latent variable model that was estimated simultaneously in all three ethnic/racial participant groups is given in Figure 2. The model hypothesizes two latent factors, one representing a latent attitude factor toward Latinos and the second representing a latent attitude factor toward Blacks. Each factor has three indicators: IAT scores, Thermometer scores, and Trait scores. As the figure indicates, these two latent variables are allowed to correlate. Additionally, residuals to the observed variables are allowed to correlate when they share the same measurement approach (i.e., Latino IAT residual with Black IAT residual), thus capturing variance specific to each way of measuring the latent attitudes.

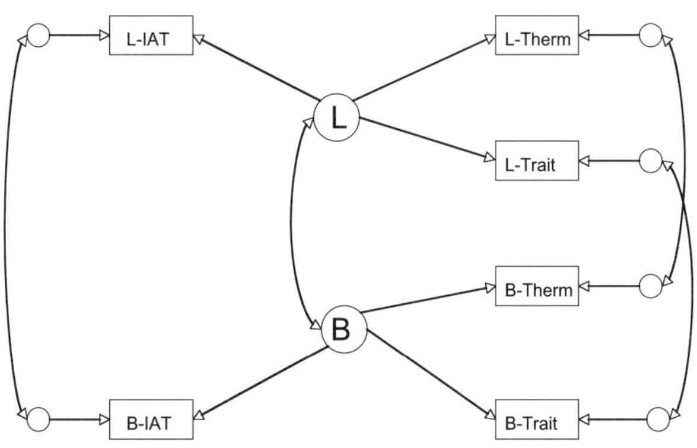


*Figure 2.* Latent variable confirmatory factor model, estimated across ethnic/racial participant groups. L, attitudes toward Latinos; B, attitudes toward Blacks; IAT, Implicit Association Test; Therm, Thermometer measure; and Trait, trait ratings.

This model was initially estimated, using AMOS (Arbuckle, 2003) to provide maximum likelihood parameter estimates, in all three participant groups, imposing no between-group constraints, that is, allowing different loadings, means (and intercepts), latent variable variances and covariances, and residual variances and covariances across groups. The metrics of the latent factors were determined by fixing the loadings of the two Trait indicators to 1.0 and estimating the variances of the latent factors. This initial unconstrained model was quite consistent with the data $\chi_{15}^2 = 23.32$, $p = .077$, RMSEA = 0.048 (90% CI: 0.000–0.085), and CFI = 0.963. The model was then re-estimated with equal indicator loadings for the three groups, thereby forcing measurement invariance across the groups. The fit of this model was also quite good, $\chi_{23}^2 = 33.85$, $p = .067$, RMSEA = 0.045 (90% CI: 0.000–0.075), and CFI = 0.952. Since this second model is a more constrained version of the first one, the difference in the resulting, $\chi^2$'s is itself distributed as a $\chi^2$ that can be used to test whether the more constrained model fits the data less well. In the present case, the difference $\chi_8^2 = 10.53$, $p > .20$, showed that one can assume that the loadings of the indicators on the two latent variables in all three groups are equivalent. This suggests that the three indicators are equally good measures of the two latent factors in all three groups.

Two further models were examined that imposed further constraints across the three groups. First, a model was estimated in which the intercepts to the indicators of the latent variables as well as the means of the latent variables were constrained to be equal across groups. This version of the model makes the strong assumption that the means of all variables are equal across the three groups. Not surprising, and consistent with the earlier results, this model was quite inconsistent with the data, $\chi_{35}^2 = 140.95$, $p < .001$. The final model, given measurement invariance (i.e., equal loadings), constrained the variance of the two latent factors and their covariance to be equal across the three groups. This model was also inconsistent with the data, $\chi_{29}^2 = 60.20$, $p < .001$. Thus we have evidence that while the loadings are equivalent for the three groups, the means and the variances/covariances of the latent factors are not.

Returning to the model that was consistent with the data in which measurement invariance was imposed, the resulting parameter estimates for the three groups are given in Table 3. These results show that all three measured variables show significant loadings on the latent variables and, importantly, the extent to which these tap the respective latent variables are invariant across groups. Second, the significant intercept differences are in line with what we have already reported: Whites show higher levels of prejudice against both groups on all three measures, while the two minority groups show less derogation of the other outgroup and relative ingroup favoritism. Unsurprisingly, all residual correlations are significant, demonstrating considerable method variance in all three measurement procedures, for all three participant groups. And importantly, although there are significant covariances between the two latent variables in all three groups, the correlations between the latent variables are, in the case of all three groups, significantly < 1.0, indicating discriminant validity. Even though each measure represents a comparison of one

© 2010 Hogrefe Publishing

*Table 3.* Parameter estimates from latent variable model: Measurement invariance

| | Participant groups | | |
|---|---|---|---|
| | African Americans | Latinos | Whites |
| *Loadings* | | | |
| Black:White trait | 1.000 | 1.000 | 1.000 |
| Black:White thermometer | 16.717* | 16.717* | 16.717* |
| Black:White IAT | 0.077* | 0.077* | 0.077* |
| Latino:White trait | 1.000 | 1.000 | 1.000 |
| Latino:White thermometer | 17.435* | 17.435* | 17.435* |
| Latino:White IAT | 0.068* | 0.068* | 0.068* |
| *Intercepts* | | | |
| Black:White trait | −0.701 | 0.383 | 0.129 |
| Black:White thermometer | −15.989 | 0.186 | 7.744 |
| Black:White IAT | 0.051 | 0.214 | 0.364 |
| Latino:White trait | −0.310 | −0.466 | 0.009 |
| Latino:White thermometer | −2.128 | −10.190 | 7.357 |
| Latino:White IAT | 0.132 | 0.009 | 0.433 |
| *Latent factor variances and covariances* | | | |
| Black factor variance | 1.471 | 0.379 | 0.728 |
| Latino factor variance | 0.501 | 0.322 | 1.392 |
| Latino-Black factor covariance | 0.400* | 0.216* | 0.538* |
| Latino-Black factor correlation | 0.466* | 0.617* | 0.534* |

*Note.* To correctly estimate the model, trait loadings were fixed at 1. $*p < .05$.

of the two minority groups with Whites, they are clearly tapping different latent constructs, assessing prejudice directed to that particular minority group.

## Discussion

The present study contributes to the debate surrounding the IAT by investigating the measure's discriminant validity, using a multi-method (implicit and explicit measures), multimeasure (Black:White and Latino:White attitudes), multigroup (African American, Latino, and White participants) approach, that allowed us to test patterns of variances and covariances that would be expected if the measures had discriminant validity. The results of this study provided strong support for the discriminant validity of the two IATs assessed here.

Similar to what was found on the explicit attitude measures, the three ethnic/racial participant groups produced significantly different IAT results that, critically, shifted radically depending on the target group. Whereas the African American participants produced the lowest level of implicit bias on the Black:White IAT and the Latino participants showed significant pro-White bias on this measure, the two groups completely switched positions on the Latino:White IAT. Confirmatory factor analysis provided additional support for the distinctiveness of the IAT measures by showing that a two-factor solution, positing separate attitudes toward Blacks and Latinos, fits the data well. Moreover this two-factor model fits the data across the three participant groups, indicating that the distinctiveness of attitudes toward Blacks and Latinos was equally valid among all three groups.

The implications of these results for attitude measurement are relatively straightforward: an IAT that contrasts the majority group (e.g., Whites) with a particular minority group (e.g., Blacks) reveals a different implicit attitude than an IAT that contrasts the same majority group with a different minority group (e.g., Latinos). It is thus important for researchers to use IATs that are specific to the particular groups of interest. With that said, one might wonder about the significance of using "Whites" or a similar group as the constant comparison. What if the comparison was Asian:Latino and Asian:Black? We did not test such comparisons in our study, however our intuition is that the comparative group context likely matters (Mitchell, Nosek, & Banaji, 2003; Turner, Hogg, Oakes, Reicher, & Wetherell, 1987) and researchers would be well advised to use group comparisons that reflect the specific social context of interest.

Before closing, two additional issues ought to be addressed. The first is the relation between implicit and explicit attitudes. The goal of the present study was to investigate the discriminant validity of IATs toward different groups, and we used explicit attitude measures to show that each IAT loaded with the explicit measures on the latent factor specific to a target group (i.e., Blacks or Latinos). Our particular interest in this model should not be taken to indicate that IAT (or implicit measures more generally) and self-report attitude measures are redundant assessments of the same construct. Rather we are simply saying that they both tell us something about the underlying evaluation of a specific social group, but there is still substantial method variance (shared residual correlations) between the implicit

 © 2010 Hogrefe Publishing

measures and the explicit measures. We refer readers interested in this aspect of the debate to other investigations designed to address the distinctiveness of implicit and explicit measures (e.g., Cunningham, Preacher, & Banaji, 2001; Nosek & Smyth, 2007).

The second issue this study addresses is the ongoing debate on whether implicit attitudes reflect "personal" or "cultural" associations. We agree with other scholars that to some extent this is a false dichotomy (e.g., Banaji, 2001). However, to the degree that "personal" is meant to imply that implicit attitudes vary from person to person in predictable and meaningful ways, our data suggest that the IAT does reveal something about a person's attitude. Although the African American, Latino, and White participants in this study all presumably are knowledgeable of American culture, there were clear differences among the three groups in their implicit attitudes, revealing personal (ingroup) as well as cultural (pro-White) preferences. Moreover, the confirmatory factor analysis showed that even within each group, the two IATs revealed sensible patterns of responses that covaried with other (explicit) measures of attitudes and distinguished between attitudes toward different groups.

In summation, prior research has shown the IAT to be a reliable measure with predictive validity. The present study provides additional support for this instrument by showing that it also possesses discriminant validity by revealing implicit associations that are specific to the target groups being evaluated, and predictably variable across participant groups. These data do not preclude the influence of other cognitive processes or meta-attitudes in the production of IAT responses. The 16% shared variance of the two IATs may be due to the fact that they had a common comparison group (Whites), or that another psychological process may have contributed to responses on both measures (e.g., ethnocentrism; see Cunningham, Nezlek, & Banaji, 2004).

However, it would be quite difficult to explain the pattern of results obtained in this study without regard to specific underlying group attitudes. The IAT is certainly not perfect, but it has proven itself to be a very useful addition to social psychology's toolbox.

## References

Arbuckle, J. L. (2003). *Amos 5.0: Update to the Amos user's guide*. Chicago: SmallWaters.

Banaji, M. R. (2001). Implicit attitudes can be measured. In H. L. Roediger III, J. S. Nairne, I. Neath, & A. M. Suprenant (Eds.), *The Nature of remembering: Essays in honor of Robert G. Crowder* (pp. 117–150). Washington, DC: American Psychological Association.

Cunningham, W. A., Nezlek, J. B., & Banaji, M. R. (2004). Implicit and explicit ethnocentrism: Revisiting the ideologies of prejudice. *Personality and Social Psychology Bulletin, 30*, 1332–1346.

Cunningham, W. A., Preacher, K. J., & Banaji, M. R. (2001). Implicit attitude measures: Consistency, stability, and convergent validity. *Psychological Science, 12*, 163–170.

Gawronski, B. (2002). What does the Implicit Association Test measure? A test of the convergent and discriminant validity of prejudice-related IATs. *Experimental Psychology, 49*, 171–180.

Greenwald, A. G., McGhee, D. E., & Schwartz, J. L. K. (1998). Measuring individual differences in implicit cognition: The Implicit Association Test. *Journal of Personality and Social Psychology, 74*, 1464–1480.

Greenwald, A. G., & Nosek, B. A. (2001). Health of the Implicit Association Test at age 3. *Zeitschrift für Experimentelle Psychologie, 48*, 85–93.

Greenwald, A. G., Nosek, B. A., & Banaji, M. R. (2003). Understanding and using the Implicit Association Test: I, An improved scoring algorithm. *Journal of Personality and Social Psychology, 85*, 197–216.

Greenwald, A. G., Poehlman, T. A., Uhlmann, E., & Banaji, M. R. (2009). Understanding and using the Implicit Association Test: III. Meta-analysis of predictive validity. *Journal of Personality and Social Psychology, 97*, 17–41.

Jost, J. T., Banaji, M. R., & Nosek, B. A. (2004). A decade of system justification theory: Accumulated evidence of conscious and unconscious bolstering of the status quo. *Political Psychology, 25*, 881–920.

Lane, K. A., Banaji, M. R., Nosek, B. A., & Greenwald, A. G. (2007). Understanding and using the Implicit Association Test: IV: What we know (so far) about the method. In B. Wittenbrink & N. Schwarz (Eds.), *Implicit measures of attitudes* (pp. 59–102). New York, NY: Guilford Press.

Mierke, J., & Klauer, K. C. (2001). Implicit association measurement with the IAT: Evidence for effects of executive control processes. *Zeitschrift für Experimentelle Psychologie, 48*, 107–122.

Mitchell, J. P., Nosek, B. A., & Banaji, M. R. (2003). Contextual variations in implicit evaluation. *Journal of Experimental Psychology: General, 132*, 455–469.

Nosek, B. A., Banaji, M. R., & Greenwald, A. G. (2002). Harvesting implicit group attitudes and beliefs from a demonstration website. *Group Dynamics, 6*, 101–115.

Nosek, B. A., Greenwald, A. G., & Banaji, M. R. (2005). Understanding and using the Implicit Association Test: II. Method variables and construct validity. *Personality and Social Psychology Bulletin, 31*, 166–180.

Nosek, B. A., Greenwald, A. G., & Banaji, M. R. (2007). The Implicit Association Test at age 7: A methodological and conceptual review. In J. A. Bargh (Ed.), *Social psychology and the unconscious: The automaticity of higher mental processes. Frontiers of social psychology* (pp. 265–292). New York: Psychology Press.

Nosek, B. A., & Smyth, F. L. (2007). A multitrait-multimethod validation of the Implicit Association Test: Implicit and explicit attitudes are related but distinct constructs. *Experimental Psychology, 54*, 14–29.

Rothermund, K., & Wentura, D. (2001). Figure-ground asymmetries in the Implicit Association Test (IAT). *Zeitschrift für Experimentelle Psychologie, 48*, 94–106.

Turner, J. C., Hogg, M. A., Oakes, P. J., Reicher, S. D., & Wetherell, M. (1987). *Rediscovering the social group: A self-categorization theory.* Oxford: Blackwell.

Irene V. Blair

Department of Psychology and Neuroscience
University of Colorado at Boulder
Boulder
CO 80309-0345
USA
Tel. +1 303 492 4563
Fax +1 303 492 2967
E-mail irene.blair@colorado.edu

© 2010 Hogrefe Publishing 

Original Article

# Prejudice Implicit Association Test Effects

## The Role of Self-Related Heuristics

Maria Popa-Roch[1] and Florian Delmas[2]

[1]Lisbon University Institute, Centre for Social Research and Intervention, Portugal
[2]Université Pierre Mendès, Grenoble, France

**Abstract.** Self-concept is accessible information that can be used when facing a demanding task. Based on findings suggesting that effects observed in Implicit Association Tests (IATs) could be partially explained by the procedural features of the task, we investigated the role of participants' self-inclusion in target categories for group IATs. We propose that IAT constraints lead participants to use self-relevant heuristics related to their membership of target categories in order to respond rapidly, which contributes to IAT group preferences. Thus positive IAT effects should dramatically diminish if participants were induced not to use self-related heuristics. Study 1 showed that when mapping outgroup names and idiosyncratic characteristics of participants onto the same category during the IAT task, the IAT effect no longer occurs. Study 2 replicated these findings when associating outgroup-participants' idiosyncratic characteristics prior to the completion of the standard IAT. Therefore inhibiting the use of self-related heuristics reduces IAT effects. The implications of our results for the construct validity of prejudice IATs are discussed.

**Keywords:** Implicit Association Test, prejudice IAT, IAT nonaffective accounts, self-related heuristics, construct validity

Self-related information seems to have a privileged position in memory. For instance, after judging whether a set of adjectives was self-descriptive, people displayed better memory for self-related items than for otherwise encoded items (self-reference effect; e.g., Rogers, Kuiper, & Kirker, 1977). Moreover it has been argued that relating information to the self can be a highly effective strategy for dealing with cognitive tasks (Greenwald & Pratkanis, 1984). The present paper aims to investigate whether the self-referenced information present in prejudice Implicit Association Test (IAT; Greenwald, McGhee, & Schwartz, 1998) can be used as a heuristic in order to perform the basic task that participants have to undertake, namely a speed categorization task. In other words, this paper seeks to scrutinize the contribution of self-related heuristics to prejudice IAT effects.

## IAT

After its publication, the IAT rapidly became the most popular implicit measure of social cognition in general, and of prejudice in particular (e.g., see Lane, Banaji, Nosek, & Greenwald, 2007). The prejudice IAT is a response-time technique thought to assess associations between two target categories (e.g., White vs. Black) and two evaluative categories (e.g., Pleasant vs. Unpleasant). The IAT computer-based task comprises two critical phases. In a race IAT, for instance, a so-called compatible phase pairs White with Pleasant and Black with Unpleasant. Conversely, an incompatible phase combines White with Unpleasant and Black with Pleasant. The difference in average speed between these two mappings (i.e., IAT effect) is believed to quantify the individual's relative preference for one target category over the other (e.g., Banaji, 2001).

A result frequently reported when using IATs to measure the prejudice of members of the majority toward a minority group is that most participants obtain positive and strong IAT effects, interpretable as prejudice against the minority group. This trend was displayed by 79% of White undergraduates who completed a White-Black IAT (Olson & Fazio, 2003), by 75% of German students in taking a German-Turkish IAT (Fiedler & Bluemke, 2005), and by 68% of a convenient sample of French participants (Popa-Roch, 2008) in a French-North African IAT.

Concerning these findings, Fiedler, Messner, and Bluemke (2006) commented that instead of reflecting alarming rates of prejudice, they could be due to confounded factors in the IAT procedure. Indeed, a growing body of research brings evidence that IAT effects are not only determined by associations between concepts but are, at least partially, rooted in nonaffective factors (e.g., see De Houwer, Teige-Mocigemba, Spruyt, & Moors, 2009).


DOI: 10.1027/0044-3409/a000007
© 2010 Hogrefe Publishing

## Alternative Accounts of the IAT Effect: Simplifying the Double Categorization Tasks

In his account entitled "mere acceptance," Mitchell (2004) proposed that the IAT binary categorization task follows an acceptance-rejection rule of decision, namely "one group of stimuli is 'accepted' as conforming to a rule while the remaining stimuli are 'rejected'" (Mitchell, 2004, p. 367). In one study, using two sets of neutral stimuli (i.e., entities that possess teeth but do not fly and entities that fly but do not possess teeth), two attitudinal IATs were designed: A Teeth-No Teeth IAT and a Flight-No Flight IAT. Significant IAT effects were obtained in favor of the "accepted" stimuli (i.e., Teeth and Flight) relative to the "rejected" ones (i.e., No Teeth and No Flight), thereby ruling out the attitudinal explanation. Importantly, Sargent, Kahan, and Mitchell (2007) found that in a racial White-Black IAT the use of a White-NonWhite decision rule favored positive IAT effects. Indeed in a Black-NonBlack version of the IAT, the preference for the White category was markedly reduced.

However, the mere acceptance account does not specify which categorical information the decision rule is based on. We maintain that in prejudice IATs, self-related information is an accessible heuristic likely to imbue the binary categorization task with the acceptance-rejection rule (i.e., the category including self is accepted, the other is rejected). This proposition integrates Mitchell's account with other nonaffective accounts more broadly based on the idea of participants simplifying the task (e.g., task-switching account; Mierke & Klauer, 2003; salience asymmetry account; Rothermund & Wentura, 2004; similarity account; De Houwer, Geldof, & De Bruycker, 2005).

In order to cope with the instruction to respond as fast as possible and with few errors, participants benefit from whatever is present in the task that facilitates the double categorization task (e.g., De Houwer et al., 2005; Mierke & Klauer, 2003; Rothermund & Wentura, 2004; Steffens & Schulze-König, 2006). For example, an attitudinal Flower-Insect IAT is particular in that it comprises a perfect confound between valence and category membership (i.e., Flower and Pleasant words are all positive in valence). The compatible phase (i.e., Flower-Positive and Insect-Negative) is simplified by recoding the two categorical dimensions in one (i.e., the valence). However, this heuristic[1] cannot be applied in the incompatible phase (i.e., Flower-Negative and Insect-Positive). The latter is accompanied by slower responses, leading to the IAT effect. Consequently, it could be theorized that rather than expressing individual differences in attitudes, IAT effects are an outcome of individual differences in using heuristics to simplify the double categorization task. We suspect that self-based mere acceptance and valence recoding combine to increase prejudice IAT effects, when participants take into account the self as information common to both one's social category membership and valence.

## Self-Related Heuristics and Prejudice IAT Effects

We propose that in prejudice IATs, simplifying the task is feasible in terms of self. On the one hand, the participant is typically a member of one of the two target categories. According to Mitchell's model, the classification of the target categories could follow the rule "Like me" versus "Unlike me." On the other hand, people evaluate the self positively (e.g., Banaji & Prentice, 1994; Greenwald & Farnham, 2000). Moreover, information related to the self tends to be highly accessible due to its constant activation (Greenwald & Pratkanis, 1984). Therefore the self forms the basis for classifying both target and valence into one single dimension, namely "Like me" (i.e., ingroup and positive) versus "Unlike me" (i.e., outgroup and negative) in the compatible assignment, but not in the incompatible one. Prejudice IAT tasks could thus be reduced to a so-called self-referenced strategy (Fiedler et al., 2006) or heuristic. In the example of the French-North African IAT that we designed for the studies developed in this paper, while performing the compatible phase a French participant could perceive that French and Pleasant are "Like me" and North African and Unpleasant are "Unlike me." As a consequence, responses in the compatible assignment are significantly facilitated, which creates apparent preferences.

Our proposition is consistent with IAT functioning as suggested by Steffens and her colleagues in order to explain self-concept IATs (Steffens, 2004; Steffens & Schulze-König, 2006): if two concepts are subjectively associated (e.g., self and consciousness), they can be reduced to one in the internal cognitive task representation.

## Overview of the Studies

We report on two studies in which we examine to what extent participants use self-related heuristics in order to cope with the demands of the IAT task. Our hypothesis is that the IAT effect should appear in favor of the category that includes the self. To explore this possibility, we reasoned that inhibiting participants' tendency to unambiguously categorize or include themselves in one of the two target categories should noticeably weaken the IAT effects.

In Study 1, participants performed one of the two modified IAT tasks. The first one contrasted the target categories

[1] Rothermund and Wentura (2004) qualify the valence use for speeding up the responses as "strategic" or "deliberate." Whether this heuristic is deliberately used or not is beyond the scope of the present paper. We use the term "recoding" or "strategy" without attributing a deliberate value. The term "heuristic" is more appropriate from our point of view.

© 2010 Hogrefe Publishing

"French and Me" to "North African." The second one contrasted the target categories "French" to "North African and Me." We expected the IAT effect to decrease when "Me" was associated with the outgroup, namely North African, but not when "Me" was associated with the self-relevant target category (i.e., the French ingroup). In Study 2, we tested the same prediction but the associations between self and ingroup or self and outgroup were manipulated more subtly, prior to a standard IAT task completion.

## Study 1

### Method

#### Participants and Design

Twenty-four female University of Grenoble psychology students participated for partial course credit. For both studies they were allegedly invited to take part in a study on "word categorization." They were randomly assigned to complete one of two versions of the IAT task, which we called "French+Me" and "North African+Me." In the former, the "French and Me" target category was represented by French names and participants' personal characteristics. In the latter, the "North African and Me" target category was exemplified by North African names and personal characteristics. Data from four foreign students were excluded, the analysis being run with the remaining 20 participants. Their mean age was 20.90 years ($SD$ = 6.17).

### Materials

The two experimental IATs, French+Me and North African+Me, were created based on a standard French-North African IAT which had as target categories French and North African. The former target category was represented by 10 typical French names (e.g., Alain and Thomas) and the other 1 by 10 typical North African names (e.g., Abdel and Hamed). The evaluative categories were Pleasant and Unpleasant, each exemplified by 10 positive words (e.g., love and friend) and 10 negative words (e.g., accident and cancer), respectively. Additionally participants were asked to provide five personal characteristics intended to represent the category "Me" in the two modified IATs: Family name, district of birth, favorite dish, favorite drink, and favorite style of music.

### Procedure

In both experiments, participants were tested individually in experimental cubicles and seated in front of a computer. The instruction and stimuli were delivered by the program *E-Prime v1.1* (Schneider, Eschman, & Zuccolotto, 2002a, 2002b). Prior to IAT completion participants were asked to respond to five personal questions. The information was inserted by the experimenter into the *E-Prime* script.

In Study 1, the two experimental IATs were structurally identical with the exception of target category labels: in the French+Me condition the target category labels were "French and Me" and "North African;" in the North African+Me condition the labels were "French" and "North African and Me." Both IATs consisted of five phases. Each phase was preceded by instructions specifying the position on the screen of the categories and their key assignment. The participants' task was to sort words by pressing the "a" (left side) and the "p" (right side) key of an AZERTY keyboard. In each trial a word was displayed in the center of the screen until a response was made. The intertrial interval was 300 ms. In the case of an incorrect response, an error feedback was given in the shape of a red "X" displayed for 300 ms. The instructions encouraged participants to respond as quickly as possible and to try to avoid errors as much as possible. In what follows we take the example of the condition French+Me for describing the IAT task. The condition North African+Me followed the same rationale, with the exception of categorizing five North African names and five personal characteristics as "North African and Me" instead of five French names and five personal characteristics as "French and Me."

The first phase required the categorizing of French names (five names) and participants' idiosyncratic characteristics (five characteristics) on one key (i.e., French and Me) and North African names (10 names) on the other key. During the second phase, participants were required to categorize words (10 positive and 10 negative) as Pleasant and Unpleasant. The third phase combined the first two phases by maintaining the same positions of categorical labels on the screen (e.g., French and Me-Pleasant/North African-Unpleasant). The fourth phase was identical to the first one, but with the positions of the category labels reversed. The fifth phase combined the fourth phase and the second one (e.g., North African-Pleasant/French and Me-Unpleasant). The simple phases (i.e., first, second, and fourth) consisted of 60 trials each and the combined ones (i.e., third and fifth) comprised 80 trials each. The order of the combined phases was counterbalanced so that half the participants completed French and Me-Pleasant/North African-Unpleasant in the third phase (and North African-Pleasant/French and Me-Unpleasant in the fifth phase) and the other half in the reverse order (i.e., North African-Pleasant/French and Me-Unpleasant in the third and French and Me-Pleasant/North African-Unpleasant in the fifth). In both experiments, after the session ended, participants were thanked and fully debriefed.

### Results

In both experiments, incorrect responses or latencies shorter than 300 ms and longer than 3,000 ms were excluded from analysis. No participants were excluded on the basis of error rates of more than 20% in the combined phases. Finally, in both studies the counterbalancing factor did not influence the IAT effect.

 © 2010 Hogrefe Publishing

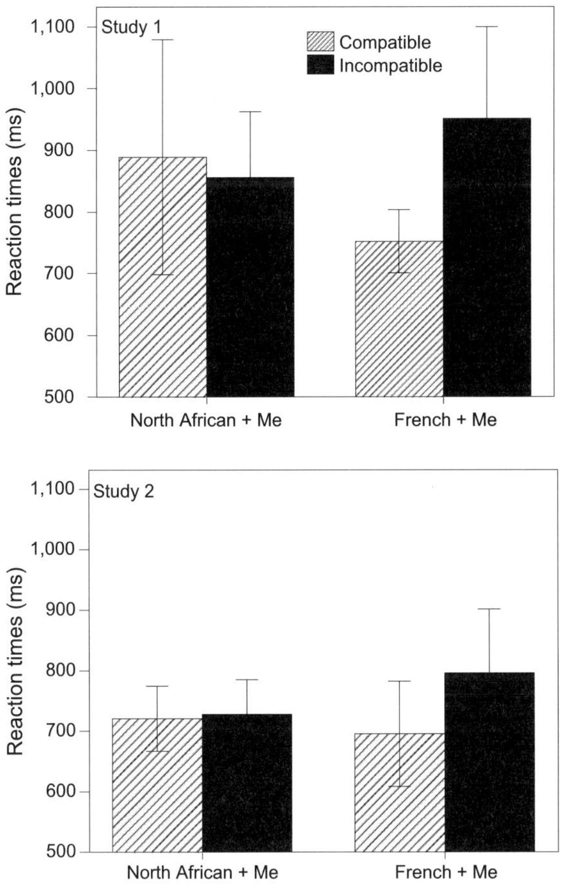


*Figure 1.* Mean reaction times in Study 1 and Study 2 for the compatible and incompatible phases as a function of the self-inclusion condition. North African+Me and French+Me refer to the conjunction between participants' idiosyncratic characteristics and North African and French target category, respectively. Error bars represent standard errors of mean values.

In Study 1, the mean percentage of incorrect responses was 4% in both compatible and incompatible phases. Both experimental IATs displayed high internal consistency (Cronbach's $\alpha$[2] being .85 for both IATs).

The reaction times[3] were subjected to a 2 (IAT version: French+Me, North African+Me) × 2 (combined phase: Compatible, Incompatible) mixed ANOVA with the second factor varying within participants. This analysis yields the predicted IAT version by combined phase interaction, $F(1, 18) = 7.21$, $p < .05$, $\eta^2 = .24$. As can be seen in Figure 1, in the French+Me condition, the French and Me-Pleasant/North African-Unpleasant assignment ($M$ = 751.80, $SD$ = 71.85) was performed significantly faster than the French and Me-Unpleasant/North African-Pleasant one ($M$ = 951.04, $SD$ = 207.33), $t(9) = 2.87$, $p < .01$, leading to a strong positive IAT effect ($M$ = 199.23, $SD$ = 219.49, $d$ = 0.90). However, in the North African+Me condition, the North African and Me-Pleasant/French-Unpleasant assignment ($M$ = 855.40, $SD$ = 149.53) was performed as fast as the North African and Me-Unpleasant/French-Pleasant one ($M$ = 888.34, $SD$ = 266.39), $t < 1$, which engendered a small negative and nonsignificant IAT effect ($M$ = −32.94, $SD$ = 162.75, $d$ = 0.20). In sum, while performing an IAT in the French+Me condition led to a large IAT effect, in the North-African+Me condition the IAT effect no longer occurred.

## Discussion

Evidence from Study 1 supports our hypothesis that inhibiting the use of self-related heuristics weakens the IAT effect. As predicted, when self and the North African category share the same response key (i.e., North African+Me condition), the two combined assignments had comparable response speed, leading to a zero IAT effect. However, when self and the French category required the same response (i.e., French+Me condition) the IAT effects were comparable to those observed in standard IATs. We believe that the French+Me condition mimicked the use of self-related heuristic by participants in conventional IAT procedures. On the contrary, in the former case we assume that simplifying the compatible task through saying that French and Pleasant are "Like me" was not possible because "North African and Me" contained elements that were "Like me" as well. In our opinion, associating the self and outgroup category inhibited the self-related heuristic used by participants for speeding up responses, especially during the compatible mapping.

Even though Study 1 yielded support for our self-related heuristic hypothesis, the procedure we used involved modifications of the IAT task and the introduction of double labels during the simple phases. The results could be due to the modified IAT structure. For instance, one could raise the possibility that the effect is driven only by the Me value (and not by the Me-Target category combination), as in a self-esteem IAT which contrasts Me and Other target categories (e.g., Greenwald & Farnham, 2000). In order to overcome these methodological limitations and to extend the evidence obtained in Study 1, we designed Study 2.

# Study 2

This study comprised two tasks, a self-target category association task and a standard French-North African IAT task. The former was meant to induce an association between self and French for half of the participants and

---

2 Cronbach's $\alpha$ was determined by computing IAT effects for each 20 stimuli. IAT effects thus obtained were considered as scale items (i.e., items represented the mean differences between the incompatible and compatible blocks).

3 Analyses were also run with log transformed reaction times. However, the results were not changed, and so rough reaction times are reported.

© 2010 Hogrefe Publishing

between self and North African for the other half. Based on our self-related heuristic hypothesis, we expected that for French participants, the IAT effect would be weakened when the self had been previously associated with the North African category rather than with the French category.

## Method

### Participants and Design

Eighteen University of Grenoble psychology students participated for partial course credit. They were randomly assigned to one of two experimental conditions, French+Me and North African+Me. Their mean age was 18.72 years ($SD = 0.95$).

## Materials

The IAT stimuli from Study 1 were used again in order to exemplify the four categories (i.e., French, North African, Pleasant, and Unpleasant). Each category was represented by 10 exemplars (cf. Study 1, Materials). Prior to the computer task, participants were asked to provide 10 personal characteristics by responding to several questions. In addition to the information solicited in Study 1, five more questions were asked (i.e., marital status, favorite color, studied subject, gender, and hobby). Supplementary material was necessary for the implementation of the experimental manipulation: 20 object names, 10 French names, and 10 North African names different from the ones used in the IAT.

## Procedure

The experimental session consisted of two phases. The two experimental conditions (i.e., French+Me and North African +Me) were induced throughout the first phase by means of a contingency learning task in the shape of a Go/No Go task. The Go/No Go task has the advantages of a consistent response key and of avoiding the left-right type of response which might interfere with the IAT response mode. While in the French+Me condition participants' self characteristics repeatedly shared the same behavioral response (i.e., the "Go" response) with French names, in the North African +Me condition self characteristics shared the same response with North African names. In the former, a prime was presented either as a French name or as an object name (e.g., desk and closet). In the latter, the prime was either a North African name or an object name. All trials had the same structure. The prime, presented for 150 ms, was followed by a fixation point (+) displayed for 1,000 ms. The target word appeared next as an object name or a personal characteristic and lasted on screen until the participant reacted, but not for more than for 600 ms. The label "Me?" was displayed in the top-center of the screen for the duration of the target display. Participants had to press the space bar if the word was a personal characteristic (i.e., Go response) or had to refrain from responding if the word was an object name (i.e., No Go response). Depending on the accuracy of the response, feedback for each trial was one of the following: "Correct," "Error," and "Error: no response." The feedback was displayed on the screen for 500 ms. Participants performed 200 Go/No Go trials. Out of these 200, half of the primes were object names and the other half were first names. When the primes were names, eight times out of ten the target was a participant's self characteristic. Conversely, when the prime was an object name, the two types of targets had the same probability of appearing (.5). This prime-target contingency was supposed to allow participants to expect that there was a good chance that a name would be followed by a personal characteristic.

The second phase of the experimental session was a French-North African standard IAT completion, identical in instructions and parameters with the IATs performed in Study 1. The difference was that the target categories were French and North African. The simple phases comprised 20 trials and the combined phases comprised 80 trials.

## Results

The mean percentage for incorrect responses was 8% in both compatible and incompatible phases. The internal consistency of the IAT was acceptable (Cronbach's $\alpha$ was .73).

The reaction times[3] were subjected to a 2 (self-associated category: French+Me and North African+Me) × 2 (combined phase: Compatible and Incompatible) mixed ANOVA with the second factor varying within participants. This analysis yielded the predicted IAT self-associated category by combined phase interaction, $F(1, 16) = 5.24$, $p < .05$, $\eta^2 = .19$. As can be seen in Figure 1, in the French+Me condition, the French-Pleasant/North African-Unpleasant mapping ($M = 695.34$, $SD = 103.76$) was performed significantly faster than the French-Unpleasant/North African-Pleasant one ($M = 796.27$, $SD = 126$), $t(7) = 4.39$, $p < .01$, leading to a strong positive IAT effect ($M = 100.93$, $SD = 65.63$, $d = 1.53$). However, in the North African+Me condition, there was no difference in response speed between the French-Pleasant/North African-Unpleasant phase ($M = 720.54$, $SD = 75$) and the French-Unpleasant/North African-Pleasant one ($M = 727.69$, $SD = 80.70$), $t < 1$, which engendered a positive but small and nonsignificant IAT effect ($M = 7.15$, $SD = 99.45$, $d = 0.07$). Therefore, Study 2 replicated the results found in Study 1, but with an unmodified IAT task.

## Discussion

The results of Study 2 give additional support to our self-related heuristic hypothesis. Repeatedly associating self and French led to significant IAT effects, while associating self and North African led to zero IAT effects. The pattern of IAT effects obtained in Study 1 was replicated through a manipulation preceding the standard IAT completion: When the self-related heuristic was inhibited, IAT effects diminished. The observed results are particularly clear in the sense that the zero-level IAT effects are obtained in both studies when self and North African are brought together.

 © 2010 Hogrefe Publishing

During the manipulation phase, the associations were induced without directly mentioning French and North African labels. Note that as the stimuli used for exemplifying French and North African categories were different in the Go/No Go and IAT tasks, it is likely that the effect was produced by the self-association with the category and not with a specific set of stimuli.

## General Discussion

The two studies reported in the current paper tested the notion of the contribution of self-related heuristics to prejudice IAT effects. Their results provide converging support for the idea that the self can be used to generate heuristics in order to deal with the task constraints, as stressed by speed-response IAT instructions. As far as we know, this is the first experimental evidence that prejudice IAT effects are at least partially grounded in self-related heuristics.

Providing initial support for our hypothesis, Study 1 showed that the tendency to perform the compatible phase faster than the incompatible one is restrained when classical IAT target categories are replaced by the dyad "French" versus "North African and Me." The zero-level bias shown in this latter case contrasts with significant positive levels of bias found when the target categories opposed during the IAT were "French and Me" versus "North African." Study 2 corroborated our expectation that inhibiting French participants' tendency to used the self as a heuristic would lead to decreased IAT effects. Hence after manipulating self-mapping with French versus North African names, zero-level IAT effects were obtained in the latter case. In accordance with our theoretical reasoning, our findings suggest that when the self is temporarily associated with the outgroup, French participants no longer take the opportunity to simplify the compatible phase to a single dimension of "Like Me"-"Unlike Me."

Overall, our results are in line with the growing body of research proposing that the remarkable size of prejudice IAT effects reported in the literature is not exclusively the result of prejudice, but also of factors that are confounded in the procedure (e.g., De Houwer et al., 2009; Fiedler et al., 2006). As such, we believe that the present data support the idea put forward by Fiedler et al. (2006) that the use of self-related heuristics (cf. "self-reference strategies") enhances the high rate of positive prejudice IAT effects commonly observed. Our reasoning was inspired by Mitchell's (2004) "mere acceptance account," which explains IAT effects through the use of an "acceptance-rejection" rule of decision when categorizing items. Our data suggested that in prejudice IATs, the self could be the criterion for setting the accepted target category. Further research should bring more direct evidence in order to establish the link between mere acceptance and self-related heuristics. However, the fact remains that using the target category closest to the self is likely to increase response efficiency, especially during the compatible phase.

If our reasoning is sound, how do we explain the IAT effects obtained in the particular case of ethnic minority participants (e.g., North Africans performing a French-North African IAT)? In their case, IAT research generally shows reduced own group preferences or even slight preferences for the outgroup (e.g., Ashburn-Nardo, Knowles, & Monteith, 2003; Dambrun, Gatto, & Roche, 2005; Nosek et al., 2007). In our opinion, self-inclusion in one of the two target categories is not clear-cut in the case of minority members, because although they are of foreign ethnic origin, they may genuinely feel a sense of belonging to the country they live in. Therefore the self-related heuristic might not be as efficient for them in the compatible phase. We can speculate that the effect would be close to what we obtained in the situation where North African and Me were brought together, namely reduced or no IAT effects.

The self-related heuristic hypothesis can contribute to understanding some surprising results in the literature. In a study using a Neonazis-Turks IAT completed by German participants, Steffens, Kirschbaum, and Glados (2008) found a preference for the Neonazi category. The stimuli exemplifying the disliked Neonazi category were traditional German first names and thus they were closer to the self-category "German" than the Turkish first names. In explaining this result the authors proposed that "(...) even if a stimulus is not positive per se, it might become so through its associations with self and the ingroup" (Steffens et al., 2008, p. 18). Because the Neonazi category could be considered as a subgroup of the German one, the self-related heuristic could have facilitated the responses in the Neonazi-Positive/Turk-Negative combination. Therefore the positive IAT effect – rather than reflecting the participants' genuine attitudes – might be the consequence of a heuristic used for responding during the task.

Although interesting and potentially challenging for the validity of prejudice IATs, some limitations of the present research should be addressed in the future. First, our findings may be due to the participants' awareness of the aim of the experiment, in other words to a demand effect. In Study 1, participants see their own characteristics mixed with North African names during the IAT, which makes the demand hypothesis plausible. However, in Study 2 this possibility is less likely because not only are participants not asked to directly associate personal characteristics and target category labels, but also the manipulation and the dependent variable measure are contained in two separate tasks. Further research should replicate these findings by using stimuli of a different nature in the manipulation phase and the IAT task. Second, whereas we reasoned that in Study 2 the Go/No Go task would create or reinforce the association between self and French versus North African, it is possible that it simultaneously modifies some other category properties such as salience (Rothermund & Wentura, 2004). Rothermund and Wentura demonstrated that IAT effects can be explained by a salience asymmetry within the two categorical dyads: the membership category is less salient than the nonmembership one, and the positive category is less salient than the negative one. It could be that in our case through repeated exposition to North African names, the latter become less salient. Therefore the reduced salience asymmetry between French and North African could explain the reduced/zero IAT effects.

© 2010 Hogrefe Publishing

To conclude, even though we cannot claim on the basis of the present research that all prejudice IAT effects are explainable in terms of self-related heuristics, their contribution is nevertheless conceivable. To date, despite significant progress in explaining the underlying mechanism of prejudice IAT effects, no existing model elucidates them entirely. We acknowledge that our self-related heuristic interpretation is yet another addition to the puzzling image of what determines the IAT effect. However, it indicates, along with other interpretations, that unambiguously interpreting IAT effects as a measure of prejudice is problematic given the present state of knowledge. This is an essential point to be considered when the IAT task is employed with a diagnostic aim, as a test for assessing individual levels of prejudice.

### Acknowledgments

This research was funded by a Rhône-Alpes Region Council (France) grant, "Prospective" Program for Ph.D. students, awarded to the first author. Maria Popa-Roch was based at Université Pierre Mendès (Grenoble, France) – Laboratoire Interuniversitaire de Psychologie (LIP) when this research was conducted.

## References

Ashburn-Nardo, L., Knowles, M. L., & Monteith, M. J. (2003). Black Americans' implicit racial associations and their implications for intergroup judgement. *Social Cognition, 21*, 61–87.

Banaji, M. R. (2001). Implicit attitudes can be measured. In H. L. Roediger & J. S. Nairne (Eds.), *The nature of remembering: Essays in honor of Robert G. Crowder* (pp. 117–150). Washington, DC: American Psychological Association.

Banaji, M. R., & Prentice, D. A. (1994). The self in social context. *Annual Review of Psychology, 45*, 297–332.

Dambrun, M., Gatto, J., & Roche, C. (2005). L'effet du statut du groupe d'appartenance sur les attitudes ethniques implicites et explicites chez les enfants. *Les Cahiers Internationaux de Psychologie Sociale, 67–68*, 65–76.

De Houwer, J., Geldof, T., & De Bruycker, E. (2005). The Implicit Association Test as a general measure of similarity. *Canadian Journal of Experimental Psychology, 59*, 228–239.

De Houwer, J., Teige-Mocigemba, S., Spruyt, A., & Moors, A. (2009). Implicit measures: A normative analysis and review. *Psychological Bulletin, 135*, 347–368.

Fiedler, K., & Bluemke, M. (2005). Faking the IAT: Aided and unaided response control on the Implicit Association Tests. *Basic and Applied Social Psychology, 27*, 307–316.

Fiedler, K., Messner, C., & Bluemke, M. (2006). Unresolved problems with the "I", the "A" and the "T": Logical and psychometric critique of the Implicit Association Test (IAT). *European Review of Social Psychology, 17*, 74–147.

Greenwald, A. G., & Farnham, S. D. (2000). Using the Implicit Association Test to measure self-esteem and self-concept. *Journal of Personality and Social Psychology, 79*, 1022–1038.

Greenwald, A. G., McGhee, D. E., & Schwartz, J. L. K. (1998). Measuring individual differences in implicit cognition: The Implicit Association Test. *Journal of Personality and Social Psychology, 74*, 1464–1480.

Greenwald, A. G., & Pratkanis, A. R. (1984). The self. In R. S. Wyer & T. K. Srull (Eds.), *Handbook of social cognition* (pp. 129–178). Hillsdale, NJ: Erlbaum.

Lane, K. A., Banaji, M. R., Nosek, B. A., & Greenwald, A. G. (2007). Understanding and using the Implicit Association Test: What we know (so far) about the method. In B. Wittenbrink & N. Schwarz (Eds.), *Implicit measures of attitudes* (pp. 59–102). New York: Guilford Press.

Mierke, J., & Klauer, K. C. (2003). Method-specific variance in the Implicit Association Test. *Journal of Personality and Social Psychology, 85*, 1180–1192.

Mitchell, C. J. (2004). Mere acceptance produces apparent attitude in the Implicit Association Test. *Journal of Experimental Social Psychology, 40*, 366–373.

Nosek, B. A., Smyth, F. L., Hansen, J. J., Devos, T., Lindner, N. M., Ranganath, K. A., et al. (2007). Pervasiveness and correlates of implicit attitudes and stereotypes. *European Review of Social Psychology, 18*, 36–88.

Olson, M. A., & Fazio, R. H. (2003). Relations between implicit measures of prejudice: What are we measuring? *Psychological Science, 14*, 636–639.

Popa-Roch, M. A. (2008). *Validation expérimentale d'une mesure implicite du préjugé: Le test d'associations implicites*. Grenoble, France: Université Pierre Mendès France Unpublished doctoral dissertation.

Rogers, T. B., Kuiper, N. A., & Kirker, W. S. (1977). Self-reference and the encoding of personal information. *Journal of Personality and Social Psychology, 35*, 677–688.

Rothermund, K., & Wentura, D. (2004). Underlying processes in the Implicit Association Test (IAT): Dissociating salience from associations. *Journal of Experimental Psychology: General, 133*, 139–165.

Sargent, M. J., Kahan, T. A., & Mitchell, C. J. (2007). The mere acceptance effect: Can it influence responses on racial Implicit Association Test. *Journal of Experimental Social Psychology, 43*, 787–793.

Schneider, W., Eschman, A., & Zuccolotto, A. (2002a). *E-prime user's guide*. Pittsburgh: Psychology Software Tools.

Schneider, W., Eschman, A., & Zuccolotto, A. (2002b). *E-prime reference guide*. Pittsburgh: Psychology Software Tools.

Steffens, M. (2004). Is the Implicit Association Test immune to faking? *Experimental Psychology, 51*, 165–179.

Steffens, M. C., Kirschbaum, M., & Glados, P. (2008). Avoiding stimulus confounds in Implicit Association Tests by using the concepts as stimuli. *British Journal of Social Psychology, 47*, 217–243.

Steffens, M. C., & Schulze-König, S. (2006). Predicting spontaneous Big Five behaviour with Implicit Association Test. *European Journal of Psychological Assessment, 22*, 13–20.

Maria Popa-Roch

Lisbon University Institute
Centre for Social Research and Intervention (CIS)
Avenida das Forças Armadas
1649-026 Lisbon
Portugal
E-mail Maria.Popa-Roch@iscte.pt

 © 2010 Hogrefe Publishing

# Prejudiced or Just Smart?

## Intelligence as a Confounding Factor in the IAT Effect

Rul von Stülpnagel and Melanie C. Steffens

Friedrich Schiller University, Jena, Germany

**Abstract.** Implicit Association Tests (IATs) are well-known measures of implicit cognition, particularly attitudes. Previous studies reported that IATs are affected by method-specific variance: IAT effects of more intelligent people may appear smaller due to their reduced task-switch costs. In contrast, based on a theoretical framework that assumes IAT effects to depend on successful recoding of the congruent IAT task, larger IAT effects are expected for more intelligent people. We tested the hypothesis that intelligence can bias IAT effects with different IATs. General processing speed was also assessed. Two studies indicated faster and more intelligent participants to have larger IAT effects in some, but not all, IATs.

**Keywords:** Implicit Association Test, method-specific variance, intelligence, cognitive skill confound, structural equation model

Implicit Association Tests (IATs; Greenwald, McGhee, & Schwartz, 1998) reflect attitudes and stereotypes in an IAT effect, that is, the reaction time differences between an incongruent (e.g., in the case of German participants: Germans/negative vs. foreigners/positive) and a congruent task (e.g., Germans/positive vs. foreigners/negative). In addition to reflecting attitudes, IAT effects can be confounded by cognitive skills (McFarland & Crouch, 2003) or general processing speed (GPS; Blanton, Jaccard, Gonzales, & Christie, 2006).

Mierke and Klauer (2003) showed that method-specific variance (MSV) in IATs is associated with disproportionally high so-called task-switch costs in the incongruent IAT task. Eliminating switch trials reduced MSV (for other attempts, see Back, Schmukle, & Egloff, 2005; Klauer, Voss, Schmitz, & Teige-Mocigemba, 2007; Teige-Mocigemba, Klauer, & Rothermund, 2008). Due to reduced task-switch costs in the incongruent task, more intelligent people should show smaller IAT effects (Klauer, Schmitz, Teige-Mocigemba, & Voss, in press).

However, the converse prediction can also be made. Performance on intelligence measures depends on task difficulty (Danthiir, Wilhelm, & Schacht, 2005), with more as compared to less intelligent people showing faster reactions in easy tasks, such as the congruent IAT task; and both groups are being equally fast in difficult tasks, such as the incongruent IAT tasks. This is in line with a recoding model that postulates the simplification of the congruent IAT task as the basis of IAT effects (Steffens et al., 2004). Thus, more intelligent people should be more able to simplify the congruent task and therefore show larger IAT effects. In order to analyze the role of intelligence in IAT effects, we conducted two experiments.

## Experiment 1

We used different measures of GPS and intelligence, and two different IATs, to test relations between IAT effects and intelligence and GPS, respectively.

### Method

*Participants* were 74 students (12 male) between 18 and 38 years ($M = 21$, $SD = 3$).

#### Materials and Procedure

The digit-symbol-test (DST; Wechsler, 1981), the *Zahlen-Verbindungs-Test* (ZVT; Oswald & Roth, 1987), two subscales of the *Leistungsprüfsystem* (LPS3 & LPS5; Horn, 1983), and the *Mehrfachwahl-Wortschatz-Intelligenztest* (MWT; Lehrl, 1977) were used as measures of intelligence. GPS was measured with latencies of three IAT practice tasks (PT1–3). Two attitude IATs (flower-insect and German-foreigner) were administered.[1]

### Results and Discussion

IAT D effects were calculated, which may reduce (for an overview, see Teige-Mocigemba et al., 2008) or even eliminate MSV (Cai, Sriram, & Greenwald, 2004). Partial correlations controlling for participant's gender (that often affects attitudes) were computed for all measures, statistical tests used $p < .05$.

[1] Details of used materials and method, and additional data are available at http://www.uni-jena.de/prof_steffens_publikationen.html.

© 2010 Hogrefe Publishing


DOI: 10.1027/0044-3409/a000008

The correlation between IAT effects was $r = .23$ ($p = .06$). GPS measures PT1–3 correlated with the insect-flower IAT effect ($rs = -.28$ to $-.30$) and the German-foreigner IAT effect ($rs = -.20$ [n.s.] to $-.31$): Faster participants showed larger IAT effects. There were no correlations between intelligence measures and the insect-flower IAT effect (all $|r| < .16$, $ps > .18$), but significant correlations between the German-foreigner IAT effect and the ZVT ($r = .26$) as well as the DST ($r = .26$), indicating more intelligent participants to show larger IAT effects. In sum, these data show evidence that IAT effects can be confounded by cognitive abilities.

## Experiment 2

Experiment 2 extended our findings with additional measures and a larger sample.

### Method

*Participants* were 148 students (21 male) from 18 to 30 years ($M = 22$, $SD = 2$).

#### Materials and Procedure

Participants again performed the ZVT and the DST and an abbreviated version of the advanced progressive matrices (APM; Raven, 1958, 1962). Average latencies of 2 IATs using the concepts as stimuli (CAT1–2, see Steffens, Kirschbaum, & Glados, 2008, for a detailed report) measured GPS. Again, a German-foreigner IAT was administered. A semantic classification IAT with the dimensions waters/plants and rivers/trees was used to exclude variance depending on individual attitude. Explicit attitudes were assessed with the Subtle and Blatant Prejudice Scale (Pettigrew & Meertens, 1995) and thermometer measures of preference for Germans over foreigners and general foreigner dislike.

### Results and Discussion

Correlations, calculated as in Experiment 1, did not emerge between the IAT effects, $r = .05$. The correlations between IAT effects and GPS were replicated (GPS1 and GPS2 with German-foreigner IAT effect: $r = -.23$ and $r = -.27$, respectively; with semantic classification IAT effect: $r = -.20$ and $r = -.13$ [n.s.], respectively). As to intelligence, we found a significant correlation between the ZVT and the German-foreigner IAT effect, $r = .18$ and two correlations with the semantic classification IAT effect (ZVT, $r = .17$ and DST, $r = .20$): More intelligent people showed larger IAT effects. Thus, even in the absence of MSV, cognitive abilities were relevant in both IAT effects. Five ($|r| > .18$) out of nine correlations between intelligence and explicit attitudes indicated more intelligent participants to have less explicit prejudice against foreigners. Higher intelligence also went along with faster GPS scores, all $|r| > .32$.

Two structural equation models showed separate significant impacts of intelligence and GPS, respectively, on the German-foreigner IAT effect in addition to the explicit attitude (Figure 1).[2] The model testing intelligence fits the data very well, $\chi^2(15) = 14.72$, $p = .47$; RMSEA = 0.00, 90% *CI* = 0.00–0.08. The model testing GPS fits the data satisfactorily, $\chi^2(11) = 15.07$, $p = .18$; RMSEA = 0.05, 90% *CI* = 0.00–0.11. In a combined model, the path weight of GPS ($-0.10$) almost vanished, whereas the effect of intelligence on the IAT effect (0.32) remained of noticeable size (n.s.). Thus, intelligence and GPS, whereas highly related, were independent determinants of the German-foreigner IAT effect. In combination, intelligence neutralized the influence of GPS, but lost some of its own weight.

## General Discussion

In two experiments faster and more intelligent participants showed larger IAT effects. Thus, individual cognitive abilities are relevant when interpreting individual IAT effect sizes. For example, assume that attitudes toward foreigners are compared for groups of different intellectual background: According to our findings, larger IAT effects would emerge for the more intelligent group, overestimating their prejudice.

Concurrently, more intelligent people showed less explicit prejudice. It seems unlikely that ambitions to control explicit prejudice differ so dramatically in a sample of students that motivation to control prejudice can explain this pattern (however, we cannot yet exclude the possibility). If, in contrast, more intelligent people are truly less prejudiced (Duckitt, 1998; Zick, 1997), these relations appear to be reversed in IAT effects.

A limitation of our findings is that it is unclear why we found correlations between IAT effects and intelligence for the German-foreigner and the semantic classification IAT, but not for the flower-insect IAT. Moreover, we could not detect significantly stronger relations between intelligence and the congruent or the incongruent IAT task. Variance in reaction times in each IAT task depends on implicit attitudes, GPS, and possibly intelligence, and it is difficult to isolate one of these factors in the presence of imperfect estimates of the others. Unfortunately, the congruent and incongruent task of the semantic classification IAT were apparently too easy or difficult, respectively, to alleviate this problem. More research is needed to pin down the exact mechanisms that determine individual IAT effects.

Although we cannot generalize from our findings to all IATs, we demonstrated that intelligence can be a methodological confound in IATs: A person with a large IAT effect may either be particularly prejudiced or particularly smart.

[2] The same models for the semantic classification IAT did not fit the data.


© 2010 Hogrefe Publishing

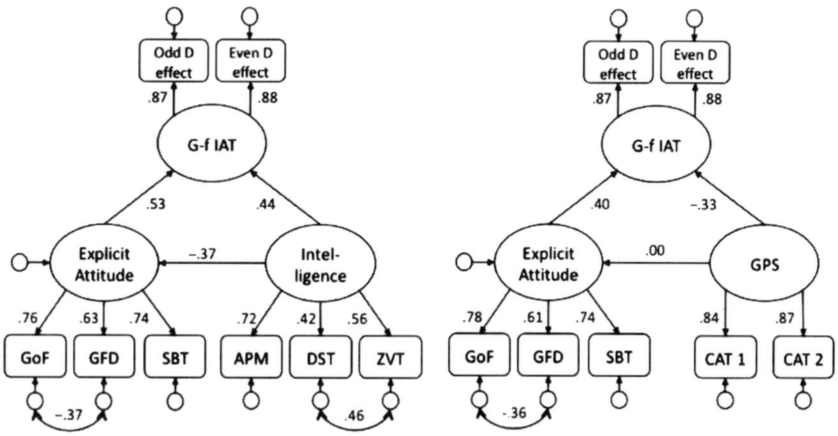


*Figure 1.* SEMs displaying influences of explicit attitudes and intelligence (left side), respectively, GPS (right side), on the German-foreigner IAT effect (G-f IAT) (Experiment 2). All path weights larger than zero are significant. GoF, preference of Germans over foreigners; GFD, general foreigner dislike; and SBT, Subtle and Blatant Prejudice Scale.


## Acknowledgments

This report was handled by editor KJJ and subject to blind review. The writing of this article was supported by a grant from the Deutsche Forschungsgemeinschaft (Ste 938/9-1). We thank Christopher Cohrs, Irena Ebert, Petra Jelenec, Nicole Kämpfe, Rainer Riemann, Jenny Roth, and Janette Schult for valuable comments and great support.


# References


Back, M. D., Schmukle, S. C., & Egloff, B. (2005). Measuring task-switching ability in the Implicit Association Test. *Experimental Psychology, 52*, 167–179.

Blanton, H., Jaccard, J., Gonzales, P. M., & Christie, C. (2006). Decoding the Implicit Association Test: Implications for criterion prediction. *Journal of Experimental Social Psychology, 42*, 192–212.

Cai, H., Sriram, N., & Greenwald, A. G. (2004). The Implicit Association Test's D measure can minimize a cognitive skill confound: Comment on McFarland and Crouch (2002). *Social Cognition, 22*, 673–684.

Danthiir, V., Wilhelm, O., & Schacht, A. (2005). Decision speed in intelligence tasks: Correctly an ability? *Psychological Science, 47*, 200–229.

Duckitt, J. (1998). *The social psychology of prejudice.* New York: Praeger.

Greenwald, A. G., McGhee, D. E., & Schwartz, J. L. K. (1998). Measuring individual differences in implicit cognition: The Implicit Association Test. *Journal of Personality and Social Psychology, 74*, 1464–1480.

Horn, W. (1983). Leistungsprüfsystem (LPS). Handanweisung (2., erweit. und verbesserte Aufl.) [Manual for the performance-test-system]. Göttingen: Hogrefe.

Klauer, C., Schmitz, F., Teige-Mocigemba, S., & Voss, A. (in press). Understanding the role of executive control in the Implicit Association Test: Why flexible people have small IAT effects. *Quarterly Journal of Experimental Psychology.*

Klauer, C., Voss, A., Schmitz, F., & Teige-Mocigemba, S. (2007). Process components of the Implicit Association Test: A diffusion-model analysis. *Journal of Personality and Social Psychology, 93*, 353–368.

Lehrl, S. (1977). Mehrfachwahl-Wortschatz-Intelligenztest (MWT-B) [Multiple-choice-vocabulary-intelligence-test]. Erlangen: Straube.

McFarland, S., & Crouch, Z. (2003). A cognitive skill confound on the Implicit Association Test. *Social Cognition, 20*, 483–510.

Mierke, J., & Klauer, C. (2003). Methodic-specific variance in the Implicit Association Test. *Journal of Personality and Social Psychology, 85*, 1180–1192.

Oswald, W. D., & Roth, E. (1987). Der Zahlen-Verbindungs-Test (2. überarbeitete und erweiterte Auflage) [Digit-connection-test]. Göttingen: Hogrefe.

Pettigrew, T. F., & Meertens, R. W. (1995). Subtle and blatant prejudice in Western Europe. *European Journal of Social Psychology, 25*, 57–75.

Raven, J. C. (1958, 1962). *Advanced progressive matrices.* London: Lewis.

Steffens, M. C., Kirschbaum, M., & Glados, P. (2008). Avoiding stimulus confounds in Implicit Association Tests by using the concepts as stimuli. *British Journal of Social Psychology, 47*, 217–243.

Steffens, M. C., Lichau, J., Still, Y., Jelenec, P., Anheuser, J., Goergens, N. K., et al. (2004). Individuum oder Gruppe, Exemplar oder Kategorie? Ein Zweifaktorenmodell zur Erklärung der Reaktionszeitunterschiede im Implicit Association Test (IAT) [Individual or group, exemplar or category? A two-factor model for explaining reaction-time differences in the Implicit Association Test (IAT)]. *Zeitschrift für Psychologie, 212*, 57–65.

Teige-Mocigemba, S., Klauer, C., & Rothermund, K. (2008). Minimizing method-specific variance in the IAT. *European Journal of Psychological Assessment, 24*, 237–245.

Wechsler, D. (1981). *Manual for the Wechsler Adult Intelligence scale – Revised.* New York: The Psychological.

Zick, A. (1997). Vorurteile und Rassismus: eine sozialpsychologische Analyse [Prejudices and racism: A socialpsychological analysis]. Berlin: Waxmann.



Rul von Stülpnagel

Institut für Psychologie
Friedrich-Schiller-Universität Jena
Am Steiger 3, Haus 1
D-07743 Jena
Germany
Tel. +49 3641 945 114
Fax +49 3641 945 112
E-mail Rul.von-Stuelpnagel@uni-jena.de


© 2010 Hogrefe Publishing

# Implicit Measures of Social Cognition

## Common Themes and Unresolved Questions

Nilanjana Dasgupta

University of Massachusetts, Amherst, MA, USA

One of the guiding themes in social psychology is that individuals' perceptions, judgments, and evaluations are often shaped by psychological processes that bypass their awareness, intention, or control and thus cannot be fully articulated in self-reports. Metaphorically speaking, these thoughts and feelings (broadly referred to as implicit social cognitions) are like a computer's operating system running invisibly in the background while other applications run in the foreground (i.e., explicit thoughts and feelings that can be articulated). In the past two decades, we as a field have been fascinated with the nature, benefits, and limits of implicit beliefs and attitudes. Empirical publications on this topic proliferated sharply after 1986 when two influential articles were published that translated theoretical ideas about less-than-conscious attitudes into empirical tests – one of these articles was by Fazio, Sanbonmatsu, Powell, and Kardes (1986), and another was by Dovidio, Evans, and Tyler (1986). These two papers gave the field initial traction into the until-then murky terrain of measurement.

In the 23 years since then, the number of implicit measures has proliferated (for a review see Dasgupta, 2004). With the growing number of measures and empirical demonstrations of implicit social cognition, numerous measurement questions have arisen: if attitudes and beliefs operate implicitly, how might we measure them? How good are these measures? How do they relate to explicit attitude measures? What do responses on these measures predict further downstream? Essentially, these are questions about specific measures' internal consistency, reliability, construct validity, discriminant validity, and predictive validity.

This special issue of *the Journal of Psychology* has gathered together a collection of empirical papers that address some of these questions. Collectively, these papers measured implicit responses toward a variety of different attitude objects – social groups, the self-concept, nonhuman living creatures, nonsocial consumer products, and risky activities. They also used at least eight different types of implicit measures (Evaluative Priming Task, Implicit Association Test – IAT, Single-Category IAT, Lexical Decision Task, Extrinsic Affective Simon Task, Evaluative Movement Assessment, Approach Avoidance Task, and Semantic Misattribution Procedure).

In this brief commentary, I will highlight three themes that emerged from this collection of papers and identify three unresolved questions in the hope that they will be pursued in the next generation of research on this topic.

### Common Themes Across Multiple Papers

#### Theme #1: Predictive Validity of Implicit Measures

Several papers in this special issue tested whether perceivers' implicit and explicit responses toward various attitude objects predict different kinds of behavior. Focusing on the self-concept, Rudolph, Schröder-Abé, Riketta, and Schütz (2010) showed that two implicit measures of self-esteem predicted indirectly assessed anxious behaviors (e.g., word use in extemporaneous speech, experimenter ratings of anxiety, and spontaneous nonverbal behavior) whereas several explicit measures of self-esteem predicted directly assessed anxious behavior (e.g., self-reported anxiety and deliberate nonverbal behavior).

In the domain of risk-taking, Dislich, Zinkernagel, Ortner, and Schmitt (2009) examined whether implicit versus explicit perceptions of risk captured by several measures would differentially predict different types of risk-taking behavior – impulsive risk-taking and deliberative risk-taking. They found that one of the implicit measures of risk-taking (but none of the explicit measures) predicted impulsive risk-taking behavior. In mirror-image fashion, two of the explicit measures of risk-taking (but none of the implicit measures) predicted reflective risk-taking behavior. Having self-control reduced the magnitude of correlation between implicit risk-taking and impulsive behavior; in an analogous fashion, having self-control amplified the magnitude of correlation between explicit risk-taking and reflective risk-taking.

In the domain of consumer attitudes and behavior, Summerville, Hsieh, and Harrington (2010) sought to identify which types of implicit reactions toward consumer products would best predict people's intentions to buy those products. They found that a measure tapping implicit emotions evoked by consumer products predicted participants' buying intentions significantly better than their general implicit attitudes

*Zeitschrift für Psychologie / Journal of Psychology* 2010; Vol. 218(1):54–57
DOI: 10.1027/0044-3409/a000009
© 2010 Hogrefe Publishing

toward those products. Interestingly, this finding nicely parallels the intergroup emotions literature which also makes the case that the specific emotions people feel toward various outgroups predict their action tendencies toward those groups better than global evaluations, probably because emotions are more tightly linked to specific goal-directed action tendencies compared to global evaluations. Summerville et al.'s (2010) finding in the consumer behavior domain provides nice convergence with the intergroup emotions work.

In the domain of arachnophobia, Reinecke, Becker, and Rinck (2010) examined whether three measures capturing people's implicit attitudes toward spiders would predict the speed with which they approached a spider. They found that for all three measures, the more people exhibited negative implicit attitudes toward spiders the more slowly they approached a spider's cage.

### Theme #2: Discriminant Validity of Implicit Measures

Blair, Judd, Havranik, and Steiner (2010) reasoned that the direction and magnitude of people's preference for particular social groups ought to depend on both: (a) people's own group membership in the target groups that are the attitude objects of interest and (b) the relative social status of the target groups. If implicit measures are to be successful at capturing people's implicit group preferences, they ought to be sensitive to participants' own social identity and the target group's status in society. Such evidence would constitute support for a measure's discriminant validity. To test this hypothesis, Blair et al. (2010) recruited three participant groups (Latinos, African Americans, and Whites) and measured their attitudes toward the same three groups using IATs. As predicted, they found that for the Black-White IAT, Black participants (a low status group) showed the least bias against their ingroup, White participants (a high status group) showed the most bias, and Latino participants (a low status group, but one whose ingroup was not represented in this IAT) exhibited implicit preferences that fell between the other two groups. The Latino-White IAT revealed mirror-image results with Latinos showing the least bias, Whites the most bias, and Black participants were in the middle. Also in support of discriminant validity, correlations between implicit and explicit measures were stronger when they focused on the same target group than when they focused on different target groups.

In part, implicit attitudes are driven by the degree to which people associate the attitude object with the self, which is a point made by Popa-Roch and Delmas (2010). The more perceivers associate the self with an attitude object (i.e., a specific target group), the more their data ought to reflect implicit liking for that attitude object (social group). To test that idea Popa-Roch and Delmas (2010) trained participants to associate the self with an outgroup and found that such training reduced implicit bias against that outgroup. Although the authors framed this finding as a methodological weakness of the IAT, which was the measure they used, I interpret this finding to be perfectly consistent with past evidence in the prejudice literature which shows that the less similar people feel toward an outgroup, the more prejudice they express. Thus, it makes perfect sense that manipulating the degree of similarity will affect the magnitude of implicit prejudice. However, as shown by the Blair et al.'s paper, besides similarity to the self, a target group's status in society also affects participants' implicit attitudes even if they do not belong to that group (and thus do not see themselves as similar to it).

### Theme #3: Implicit and Explicit Attitudes Represent Two Independent Constructs, Not One

Coming at this issue from different angles, several of the papers in this collection made the point that implicit and explicit measures capture independent (but partially correlated) psychological constructs. For example, in the domain of self-esteem, using structural equation modeling Rudolph et al. (2010) showed that implicit and explicit self-esteem were best represented as two independent latent constructs (not as a single construct) that predicted indirect and direct types of anxious behavior, respectively. Using different methodology Summerville, Dislich, Reinecke, and their respective colleagues came to the same conclusion after finding that correlations between implicit attitudes and subtle behaviors are stronger than those between implicit attitudes and overt behaviors. Similarly, correlations between explicit attitudes and overt behaviors are stronger than those between explicit attitudes and indirect behaviors.

## The Next Generation of Unresolved Questions

These papers also surface some of the unresolved questions about implicit measures in particular and implicit social cognition more generally. Below, I highlight three such questions in the hope that they will be productive avenues of future research.

### When Do Implicit Measures of the Same Attitude Object Hang Together Versus When Are They Uncorrelated?

Several of the reported studies used multiple implicit measures to tap participants' sentiments toward the same attitude object. Results showed that these implicit measures were either only modestly correlated or, in some cases, completely uncorrelated (e.g., Dislich et al., 2010; Reinecke et al., 2010; Rudolph et al., 2010; Summerville et al., 2010). This raises the question: does the weak-to-null correlation capture measurement differences or meaningful theoretical differences between implicit measures? This question is an important one that needs to be systematically addressed in the future.

© 2010 Hogrefe Publishing

## The Connection Between Implicit Measures and The Definition of Implicit Social Cognition

All the papers in this special issue used implicit measures that were based on response latency. This type of measurement assessing how quickly one concept is associated with a particular attribute, evaluation, etc., rests on the idea that implicit attitudes/beliefs are thoughts or evaluations that pop into mind quickly and automatically without control or intention. But the logic driving these reaction time-based measures is typically agnostic about whether or not participants are aware of the attitudes under investigation while completing the task. The assumption is that because these tasks require rapid responses, even if participants become semi-aware of the attitude being measured, they cannot easily control their responses.

One fruitful avenue of future research would be to focus more attention on developing and testing tasks that measure implicit attitudes and beliefs without participants being aware of the object under investigation. After all, an integral part of the definition of implicit attitudes that tends to be neglected in recent empirical work refers to *thoughts and feelings that operate without perceivers' awareness* (Banaji & Dasgupta, 1998; Bargh, 1994; Greenwald & Banaji, 1995; Nisbett & Wilson, 1977). One might argue that in most of the studies in this special issue participants may have been reasonably aware of their responses although they may not have had the opportunity to control them. Would these results look similar or different had these studies used alternative implicit measures that tapped participants' sentiments without their awareness (vs. their control)?

## Does the Use of Specific Attitude Objects Moderate the Robustness of Results Yielded by Implicit Measures?

Collectively, the present studies measured implicit reactions toward a vastly diverse array of attitude objects – social groups, the self-concept, nonhuman living creatures, consumer products, and risky activities. How well each implicit measure performs is likely to be influenced, at least in part, by the type of attitude object that was the focus of this investigation. Attitude objects that evoke highly elaborated versus weakly elaborated thoughts; that are important versus unimportant to the self; that arouse high versus low social desirability concerns or strong versus weak emotions are all likely to moderate and change the performance of implicit measures in terms of their predictive validity and convergent validity with explicit measures. This issue has only been examined in two empirical papers specifically in relation to the IAT (Greenwald, Poehlman, Uhlmann, & Banaji, 2009; Nosek, 2005) and needs to be investigated for other implicit measures as well.

In conclusion, this special issue with its collection of empirical papers offers a nice resting place to stop, look back, and reflect on what we know (so far) about implicit measures and the attitudes and beliefs they seek to capture and what there is yet to learn.

## References

Banaji, M. R., & Dasgupta, N. (1998). The consciousness of social beliefs: A program of research on stereotyping and prejudice. In V. Y. Yzerbyt, G. Lories, & B. Dardenne (Eds.), *Metacognition: Cognitive and social dimensions*. Great Britain: Sage.

Bargh, J. A. (1994). The four horsemen of automaticity: Awareness, intention, efficiency, and control in social cognition. In R. S. Wyer Jr. & T. K. Srull (Eds.), *The handbook of social cognition: Basic processes*. (Vol. 2, pp. 1–40). Hillsdale, NJ: Erlbaum.

Blair, I. V., Judd, C. M., Havranek, E. P., & Steiner, J. F. (2010). Using community data to test the discriminant validity of ethnic/racial group IATs. *Zeitschrift für Psychologie / Journal of Psychology, 218*, 36–43.

Dasgupta, N. (2004). Implicit ingroup favoritism, outgroup favoritism, and their behavioral manifestations. *Social Justice Research, 17*, 143–169.

Dislich, F. X. R., Zinkernagel, A., Ortner, T. M., & Schmitt, M. (2009). Convergence of direct, indirect, and objective risk taking measures in gambling: The moderating role of impulsiveness and self-control. *Zeitschrift für Psychologie / Journal of Psychology, 218*, 20–27.

Dovidio, J. F., Evans, N., & Tyler, R. B. (1986). Racial stereotypes: The contents of their cognitive representations. *Journal of Experimental Social Psychology, 22*, 22–37.

Fazio, R. H., Sanbonmatsu, D. M., Powell, M. C., & Kardes, F. R. (1986). On the automatic activation of attitudes. *Journal of Personality and Social Psychology, 50*, 229–238.

Greenwald, A. G., & Banaji, M. R. (1995). Implicit social cognition: Attitudes, self-esteem, and stereotypes. *Psychological Review, 102*, 4–27.

Greenwald, A. G., Poehlman, T. A., Uhlmann, E. L., & Banaji, M. R. (2009). Understanding and using the Implicit Association Test: III. Meta-analysis of predictive validity. *Journal of Personality and Social Psychology, 97*, 17–41.

Nisbett, R. E., & Wilson, T. D. (1977). Telling more than we can know: Verbal reports on mental processes. *Psychological Review, 84*, 231–259.

Nosek, B. A. (2005). Moderators of the relationship between implicit and explicit evaluation. *Journal of Experimental Psychology: Learning, Memory, and Cognition, 134*, 565–584.

Popa-Roch, M., & Delmas, F. (2010). Prejudice Implicit Association Test effects: The role of self-related heuristics. *Zeitschrift für Psychologie / Journal of Psychology, 218*, 44–50.

Reinecke, A., Becker, E. S., & Rinck, M. (2010). Three indirect tasks assessing implicit threat associations and behavioral response tendencies: Test-retest reliability and validity. *Zeitschrift für Psychologie / Journal of Psychology, 218*, 4–11.

Rudolph, A., Schröder-Abé, M., Riketta, M., & Schütz, A. (2010). Easier when done than said! Implicit self-esteem predicts observed or spontaneous behavior, but not self-reported or controlled behavior. *Zeitschrift für Psychologie / Journal of Psychology, 218*, 12–19.

Summerville, A., Hsieh, B., & Harrington, N. (2010). The divergence of implicit and explicit consumer evaluations: A multimeasure investigation. *Zeitschrift für Psychologie / Journal of Psychology, 218*, 28–35.

 © 2010 Hogrefe Publishing

Nilanjana Dasgupta

Department of Psychology
University of Massachusetts
Tobin Hall
135 Hicks Way
Amherst MA 01003 USA
Tel. +1 413 545 0049
Fax +1 413 545 0996
E-mail dasgupta@psych.umass.edu

© 2010 Hogrefe Publishing

# Calls for Papers

## "Torture"

### A Topical Issue of the *Zeitschrift für Psychologie / Journal of Psychology*

Guest Editors: Thomas Elbert, Roland Weierstall (University of Konstanz, Germany), and Andreas Maercker (University of Zurich, Switzerland)

Torture is supposed to have a devastating impact on individual as well as on public health, as it causes serious damage to the mental and physical health. However, research on this topic is rare, yet seldom empirical. For the topical issue we invite submissions of empirical as well as theoretical papers that relate to the psychology of torture and instrumental violence. It aims to bring together promising work on behavioral, neuropsychological, and stress-mediated physiological consequences of torture to approach this topic from different perspectives. All areas that increase insight into the understanding of the consequences of torture will be considered. We explicitly encourage the submission of studies that investigate the mental health status of torture survivors or explore possibilities for treatment.

The submission encompasses two phases. Authors are requested to submit only the abstracts of their proposed papers first. In a second phase, authors that are requested to submit full papers should then do so for full peer review. Manuscripts can be submitted electronically to: roland.weierstall@uni-konstanz.de.

**Deadline for submission of abstracts is May 15, 2010.**

**Deadline for submission of full papers is August 30, 2010.**

For additional information, please contact: Roland Weierstall (roland.weierstall@uni-konstanz.de).

The topical issue will be published as Issue 2 (2011).

The *Zeitschrift für Psychologie / Journal of Psychology* was founded in 1890 and is the second oldest psychology journal in the world. One of the founding editors was Hermann Ebbinghaus. Since 2007, it is published in English and is devoted to publishing topical issues that provide state-of-the-art reviews of current research in psychology.

Guidelines for article preparation:

- only English-language submissions can be considered;
- all papers must be original contributions (they may not have been published previously or currently be under review for publication elsewhere);
- regular articles must not exceed 45,000 characters in length, including references and tables;
- reference citations in the text and in the reference list should be in accordance with the principles set out in the Publication Manual of the American Psychological Association (6th ed.) – see also any recent issue of the journal;
- submissions should be typeset in a standard font such as Times/Times New Roman 12 pt, with a margin of 3 cm;
- illustrations and tables must be submitted on a separate page.

For detailed author guidelines, please see the journal's website at www.hogrefe.com/journals/zfp/.


DOI: 10.1027/0044-3409/a000010
© 2010 Hogrefe Publishing

# "Prospective Memory"

## A Topical Issue of the *Zeitschrift für Psychologie / Journal of Psychology*

Guest Editor: Rebekah E. Smith
(University of Texas, San Antonio, TX, USA)

How do we remember to perform an intended action when time and activities intervene between the formation of the intention and an opportunity to perform the intended action? This particular function of memory is called prospective memory. The ability to perform these tasks is a fundamental aspect of our daily lives. For instance, individuals who cannot remember to turn off the stove or take medication will require daily assistance. In the last two decades there has been an increased focus on prospective memory. Much of the increased interest can be attributed to the publication of a study by Einstein and McDaniel in 1990 that laid the cornerstone for the expansion of prospective memory research through the introduction of a laboratory paradigm for investigating prospective memory. In addition, Einstein and McDaniel's study spurred an early and continuing interest in adult age differences in prospective memory.

In the spirit of Einstein and McDaniel's (1990) study, the topical issue of the *Zeitschrift für Psychologie / Journal of Psychology* invites submissions of papers that either use alternative paradigms or analytic methods and/or papers that focus on group or individual differences in prospective memory across a variety of domains. The purpose of the issue is to highlight recent developments in the area of prospective memory research and to draw attention to the broad array of factors that can influence prospective memory performance both in and out of the laboratory. Contributions from all areas of prospective memory research are welcome, with particular interest in contributions that focus on new paradigms, analytic methods, and the investigation of factors that influence prospective memory performance, such as:

- new paradigms for investigating prospective memory
- novel extensions or applications of existing techniques
- mathematical modeling and other alternative data-analytic approaches
- meta-analyses
- investigations of age difference in childhood and/or adulthood
- effects of noncognitive factors such as personality and motivation
- the role of lifestyle factors such as education, employment, and engagement
- the effects of physical or mental illness, disease, or injury.

### References

Einstein, G. O., & McDaniel, M. A. (1990). Normal aging and prospective memory. *Journal of Experimental Psychology: Learning, Memory, and Cognition*, *16*, 717–726.

There is a two-stage submission process. Initially, authors are requested to submit only abstracts of their proposed papers. Authors requested to submit full papers should then do so. All papers will undergo full peer review. Abstracts/manuscripts can be submitted electronically to Rebekah E. Smith (rebekah.smith@utsa.edu).

**Deadline for submission of abstracts is July 15, 2010.**

**Deadline for submission of full papers is November 15, 2010.**

For additional information, please contact:
Rebekah E. Smith (rebekah.smith@utsa.edu).

The journal seeks to maintain a short turnaround time, with the final version of the accepted papers being due by March 15, 2011. The topical issue will be published as issue 3 (2011).

The *Zeitschrift für Psychologie / Journal of Psychology* was founded in 1890 and is the second oldest psychology journal in the world. One of the founding editors was Hermann Ebbinghaus. Since 2007, it is published in English and is devoted to publishing topical issues that provide state-of-the-art reviews of current research in psychology.

Guidelines for article preparation:

- only English-language submissions can be considered;
- contributions must be original (not published previously or currently under review for publication elsewhere);
- regular articles should not exceed 45,000 characters and spaces in length, including references, figures, and tables (allowances for figures and tables should be deducted on the basis of size – approximately 1,250 characters for a quarter-page figure/table);
- reference citations in the text and in the reference list should be in accordance with the principles set out in the *Publication Manual of the American Psychological Association* (6th ed.) – see also any recent issue of the journal;
- submissions should be typeset in a standard font such as Times / Times New Roman 12 pt, with a margin of 3 cm;
- illustrations and tables must be submitted on a separate page.

For detailed author guidelines, please see the journal's website at www.hogrefe.com/journals/zfp/.

© 2010 Hogrefe Publishing


DOI: 10.1027/0044-3409/a000011

# Implicitly. Measuring and managing social bias

implicitly

**We all have unconscious social biases but, until now, we haven't been able to identify and measure these. Now things have changed.**

Implicitly is a range of tests which predict the risk of discriminatory behaviour against specific social groups including gender, age, ethnic origin, sexual orientation and disability.

Implicitly is of value across clinical, forensic and business settings – whenever you need to find out about the biases and associations a person holds (of which they may be unaware). Typically these are inaccessible through traditional means.

Individuals benefit greatly from the insight gained when used within an assessment or development programme and organisations can flourish when Implicitly is used as part of an organisational audit of social attitudes.

By introducing Implicitly, you'll be encouraging a more inclusive organisation which enjoys engagement from everyone.

**For more information, visit www.hogrefe.co.uk**

HOGREFE

**Contact us on +44 (0) 1865 402900 or info@hogrefe.co.uk**

HG0009